VOLUME III

# Dining In–Chicago
# COOKBOOK

A Collection of Gourmet Recipes for Complete Meals
from the Chicago Area's Finest Restaurants

BARBARA
GRUNES

Foreword by
IRV KUPCINET

Peanut Butter Publishing
Mercer Island, Washington

## Titles In Series

Dining In–Baltimore
Dining In–Boston
Dining In–Chicago, Vol. I
Dining In–Chicago, Vol. II
Dining In–Chicago, Vol. III
Dining In–Dallas
Dining In–Denver
Dining In–Hawaii
Dining In–Houston, Vol. I
Dining In–Houston, Vol. II
Dining In–Kansas City
Dining In–Los Angeles
Dining In–Manhattan
Dining In–Milwaukee
Dining In–Minneapolis/St. Paul, Vol. I
Dining In–Minneapolis/St. Paul, Vol. II
Dining In–Monterey Peninsula
Dining In–Philadelphia
Dining In–Phoenix
Dining In–Pittsburgh
Dining In–Portland
Dining In–St. Louis
Dining In–San Francisco
Dining In–Seattle, Vol. I
Dining In–Seattle, Vol. II
Dining In–Seattle, Vol. III
Dining In–Sun Valley
Dining In–Toronto
Dining In–Vail
Dining In–Vancouver B.C.
Dining In–Washington, D.C.

Cover photograph by Kenneth Redding
Edited by Charles Malody
Production and illustrations by Carol Naumann
Typesetting by Mac White-Spunner

Copyright© 1983 by Peanut Butter Publishing, 2445 76th Avenue S.E., Mercer Island, WA 98040 (206)236-1982
All rights reserved. Printed in the United States of America

ISBN 0-89716-125-4

# Contents

| | |
|---|---|
| *Foreword* | *v* |
| *Introduction* | *vii* |
| Arnie's | 1 |
| The Bakery | 11 |
| Cape Cod Room | 21 |
| The Chestnut Street Grill | 29 |
| Chez Paul | 37 |
| The Consort | 47 |
| Cricket's | 53 |
| L'Escargot | 63 |
| George's | 71 |
| Gordon | 77 |
| House of Hunan | 87 |
| Jovan | 99 |
| Lexander | 107 |
| Meson del Lago | 119 |
| Nick's Fishmarket | 127 |
| M. Foley's Printer's Row | 135 |
| Sogni Dorati | 143 |
| Tango | 153 |
| Three Happiness | 161 |
| Truffles | 169 |
| Yoshi's Café | 177 |
| *Recipe Index* | *185* |

## FOREWORD

Chicago is energy. "The city of the big shoulders" as Carl Sandberg named us, is a strong, dynamic place on the prairie.

Barbara Grunes knows the city, its dynamism, its neighborhoods. She has singled out restaurants where Chicagoans and their visiting friends dine in ecstasy, for the city on Lake Michigan also knows how to enjoy itself.

This book lists the fine restaurants that are the equal of any in this country, places where one can feel those special qualities that make up this dynamic city.

Irv Kupcinet

## INTRODUCTION

Chicago, the capital of the mid-west, is a major cosmopolitan city and a mecca as a cultural center. It is now celebrating its 150th anniversary. Chicago has museums, theatre, opera, shopping centers, historic landmarks, a handsome lakefront and fine restaurants, all part of the Chicago tradition. Imaginative restaurateurs from the world over have brought to Chicago their ethnic traditions in foods, haute cuisine and now the emerging "American style" of cooking. Food is the symbolic force that captures the true sense of Chicago's people.

The French are justly proud of the meticulous care that they bestow on meal preparation; only the freshest ingredients are thoughtfully prepared to perfection. Here in Chicago you can experience the same care, not only in French food, but also in Mexican, Greek, Chinese, the new American style and Nouvelle cuisine. Because you cannot always dine out, some of the finest chefs in the area have generously agreed to allow you to peer over their shoulders, into their kitchens. You can have foods that appear on their menus by preparing these taste-tempting delectable dishes yourself.

*Dining In–Chicago, Volume III* enables the reader to accomplish two things. First, to become aware of the variety of dining available in the Chicago area. Second, to sample some of the best tastes that they have to offer at home. This process will enrich one's repetoire.

It is with the greatest pride that I present *Dining In–Chicago, Volume III*. I know that the recipes you are about to enjoy will bring to you and your family or guests as much pleasure as they provide to patrons of these distinguished restaurants. Whatever your culinary tastes, Chicago truely remains, "Your kind of town".

Barbara Grunes

# ARNIE'S

*Dinner for Six*

*Vegetable Soufflé*

*Cauliflower Soup*

*Arnie's Salad*

*Steamed Salmon and Scallops with Capellini*

*Chocolate Velvet Cake*

*Arnold Morton, Owner*

*Jörg Liniper, Chef*

## ARNIE'S

Arnie's restaurant has continued to be a most unique dining spot for almost ten years. It is centrally located in the middle of the active area of Rush Street in the Newberry Plaza. The lavish interior designed by Jim Miller contains stained glass, gilded mirrors, handsome exotic plants, neon, all brought together in a profusion of styles in four rooms. The decor has a backdrop of an enormous five story atrium. After all these years Arnie's is still a temple of beauty and excitement.

Arnie Morton is no stranger to the restaurant business. He was director of the hotel and club division of Playboy Enterprises. Ten years ago he opened the first of his fine restaurants, Arnie's.

Manager Barry Devine says, "We try to serve what people are interested in eating. We use a fresh new approach, most recently it is with pasta and fresh fish. A selection of grilled tuna with a light butter sauce seasoned with fresh chives, is a good example. We try to appeal to a Chicago market by using the best quality foods that are readily available," he continued.

Chef Jörg Limper was trained in Europe. He is also responsible for recipe development. His innovative cuisine combines with Jim Miller's design and Arnie Morton's experience to make Arnie's a restaurant of casual elegance and fun.

1030 North State Street

## ARNIE'S

### VEGETABLE SOUFFLE

1 pound fresh spinach
6 medium eggs
1 cup heavy cream
  Salt and pepper, to taste
  Nutmeg and sugar, to taste
3 fresh tomatoes, blanched peeled, and seeded
4 ounces imported Swiss Cheese, grated

1. Preheat oven to 350°. Butter a 4- to 4½-cup terrine.
2. Blanch spinach. Remove from heat and drain in a colander, making sure to squeeze out all moisture. Then chop spinach in food processor fitted with steel blade. Add 2 eggs and ⅓ cup heavy cream and process. Add small amounts of salt, pepper, nutmeg and sugar. Set aside.
3. Reduce tomatoes in stainless steel or porcelain pan until all liquid evaporates (paste consistency).
4. Again fit processor with steel blade. Process tomatoes, 2 eggs, and ⅓ cup heavy cream. Add small amount of salt, pepper, nutmeg and sugar. Set aside.
5. Mix Swiss cheese, 2 eggs and remaining ⅓ cup heavy cream. Again add small amounts of salt, pepper, nutmeg and sugar. Stir to combine.
6. Put terrine in roasting pan filled with approximately two inches of water. Add spinach mixture to terrine and bake for 20 minutes. Then add tomato mixture on top of baked spinach mixture and bake for 25 minutes or until slightly firm. Add cheese mixture and bake for 35 minutes or until firm.
7. Cool, unmold, cut and serve.

*Prepare the tomato and cheese layers while the spinach layer bakes.*

## ARNIE'S

## CAULIFLOWER SOUP

- ¼ cup Spanish onion, chopped
- 1 ounce clarified butter
- ¼ cup diced leek
- ½ pound raw baking potato, peeled and diced
- ¼ cup diced celery
- ¼ teaspoon salt
- Pinch ground white pepper
- ½ tablespoon chicken base
- 1 large head or 2 small heads cauliflower, broken into small florets
- 1 quart water
- 1¼ cups heavy cream
- 1 tablespoon butter

1. Sauté onions in a large pan in clarified butter until onions are transparent.
2. Add leek, diced potatoes and celery; sauté until potatoes are tender.
3. Add salt, pepper and chicken base; mix well.
4. Add cauliflower, cover pan loosely and steam vegetables for approximately 15 minutes, stirring occasionally.
5. Add water, reduce heat and simmer approximately 45 minutes to 1 hour.
6. Scald cream in separate saucepan; reserve.
7. Strain vegetables and reserve liquid.
8. In a food processor fitted with steel blade or in a blender, puree vegetables and a small amount of the liquid.
9. Add puree and remaining liquid to scalded cream and heat through.
10. Finish soup with 1 tablespoon butter on top to prevent skin from forming. Serve in heated bowls.

*To clarify butter, melt butter in a heavy saucepan and then allow to cook. Skim off the white foam that may form on the surface. The remaining yellow butter is the clarified butter.*

# *Arnie's*

## ARNIE'S SALAD

1 head Iceberg lettuce, cut in large pieces
1 head Romaine lettuce, cut in large pieces
ARNIE'S SALAD DRESSING
1 hard-boiled egg, chopped
12 flat anchovy filets, drained

1. Combine lettuces and toss with dressing.
2. Serve on large plate. Top with chopped egg and anchovy fillets, criss-crossed.

## ARNIE'S DRESSING

1 cup heavy mayonnaise
⅔ cup sour cream
⅓ cup Blue cheese crumbs
2 tablespoons buttermilk
1 ounce Durkel Sandwich Sauce
Lawry's Seasoned Salt, to taste
Ground black pepper, to taste

1. Combine all ingredients in a mixing bowl and mix thoroughly by hand.
2. Refrigerate until ready.

## *Arnie's*

### STEAMED SALMON AND SCALLOPS WITH CAPELLINI

- 1 pound fresh imported Capellini pasta
- 1 stalk Swiss chard or spinach
- 18 fresh sea scallops
- 6 (4 to 6 ounce) salmon fillets, skinned
- 2 tablespoons unsalted butter
- ½ cup fresh leek, julienned
- 1 large tomato, seeded and julienned
- Salt and pepper, to taste
- BEURRE ROUGE

1. Cook Capellini in salted boiling water until al dente. Rinse in warm water; set aside.
2. Cut off green leafy ends of Swiss chard stalk and blanch quickly. Rinse in cold water. Wrap scallops in Swiss chard, one per leaf.
3. In a large steamer, add salmon fillets and wrapped scallops. Cover and cook until salmon are opaque, approximately 4 to 5 minutes.
4. While fish is steaming, melt 2 tablespoons butter in a large skillet over medium heat. Add leek and sauté until tender. Add julienne of tomato and cooked pasta. Toss all together until warm and evenly coated with butter. Season with salt and pepper.
5. Divide pasta evenly among six warm plates. Place one cooked salmon fillet in center of each plate. Wrap each fillet with 2 ounces of Beurre Rouge.
6. Garnish each plate with three wrapped scallops.

# Arnie's

### *BEURRE ROUGE*

- 2 cups red wine (Burgundy or Zinfandel)
- 1 tablespoon red wine vinegar
- 1 teaspoon chopped shallots
- 1 pound unsalted butter
- Salt and pepper, to taste

1. In an enamel or stainless steel pan, reduce red wine, red wine vinegar and shallots to ¼ cup liquid.
2. While reducing liquid, cut butter into teaspoon-size bits. Remove reduced liquid from heat and whisk in butter, one piece at a time, until all butter is incorporated. Season with salt and pepper.
3. Strain sauce and reserve in warm water bath until needed.

*Leeks are a favorite in France. They are grown with earth mounded around the bottom, therefore they get very sandy. The trapped dirt should be removed by careful washing. The green portion should be saved for use in soups.*

## ARNIE'S

### CHOCOLATE VELVET CAKE

| | |
|---|---|
| 8 tablespoons butter | 2 cups heavy cream |
| 24 ounces semi-sweet chocolate | 3 egg whites |
| | ¼ cup Confectioner's sugar |
| 3 egg yolks | ⅛ teaspoon salt |
| ½ tablespoon instant coffee | ⅓ cup praline paste |
| 2 ounces Kirschwasser | FROSTING |
| 2 ounces dark Jamaican rum | CHOCOLATE GENOISE BASE |
| 2 ounces dark Creme de Cacao | |

1. Melt butter and semi-sweet chocolate in the top of a double boiler. Allow to cool so as to mix with other ingredients. Then stir in egg yolks.
2. Dissolve instant coffee in Kirschwasser, dark rum and creme de cacao in a large bowl.
3. Whip cream in chilled mixing bowl until peaks form; set aside.
4. In another bowl beat egg whites and salt until soft peaks form. Sprinkle egg whites with sugar and continue beating until stiff peaks form.
5. Fold beaten egg whites into chocolate and mix thoroughly without over beating. Add praline paste and blend in. Then fold whipped cream into mixture.
6. Pour into springform pans containing Chocolate Genoise base. Chill.
7. Unmold, frost and serve.

## Arnie's

### CHOCOLATE GENOISE

6 eggs, room temperature
1 cup extra fine sugar
1 teaspoon vanilla

1 cup cake flour
3 tablespoons powdered chocolate
¼ cup butter, melted

1. Preheat oven to 350°.
2. Beat eggs and sugar in large bowl with electric mixer at high speed until mixture is stiff, about 20 to 30 minutes. Blend in vanilla.
3. Sift cake flour together with chocolate.
4. Alternately fold 3 tablespoons of flour mixture and 2 tablespoons of the cooled melted butter into the batter.
5. Grease two 10-inch cake pans. Pour batter equally into both and bake for 30 to 35 minutes.

### FROSTING

6 ounces semi-sweet chocolate, melted
1¼ cups Confectioner's sugar, sifted

4 to 6 tablespoons half and half

Combine all ingredients in a large bowl; blend until smooth.

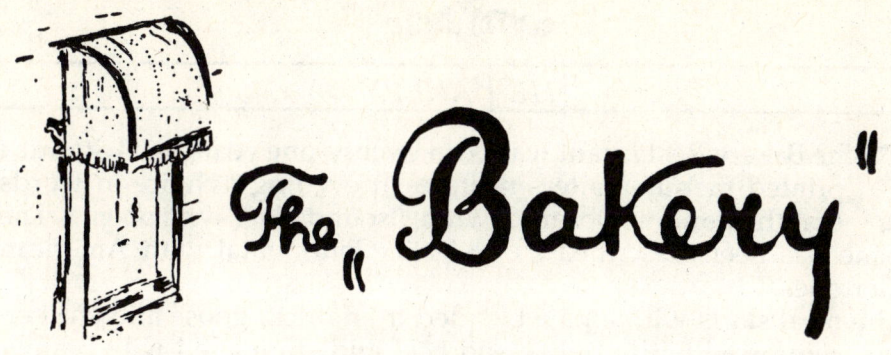

# The "Bakery"

*Dinner for Eight*

Stockyard Inn Marinated Beef

Cauliflower Soup

Baked Grouper with Sauce Louis and Hot Herb Butter

Celery Knob Remoulade

Brownie Bottom Bourbon Pie

Chocolate Sauce

Wine:

With Appetizer: Chandon Brut, Napa Valley

With Grouper: B.V. Pinot Chardonnay

With Dessert: Tokaji Aszu 4 Puttonos (Hungary)

Louis Szathmary, Owner/Chef

## The Bakery

The Bakery Restaurant was born twenty-one years ago without a printed menu. Waiters recite each evening's choice in words that the London Observer wrote "sound like a lyric poem." The cuisine has been described as "eclectic Continental with American undertones."

The meal starts with a pâté blended from duck, goose and chicken livers, reinforced with poultry and beef and stimulated with brandy and spices. Soup comes from a simmering pot of stock, never just water. It could be cream of potato, or asparagus, or kohlrabi, or fresh tomato with herbs. Salad emerges from a bowl of greens with dressings that never saw a bottle; or it could be a distinctive celery root salad with champagne mayonnaise. For the heart of the meal, Beef Wellington and Roast Duckling are consistently offered. A half-dozen other choices may be had, varying by day, by week, by season and by just plain inspiration. Each comes with a vegetable selected because it is seasonal, the most fresh, and best mated to the main course—a piquant ratatouille, dilled squash with sour cream, or cauliflower polonaise. The desserts provoke sighs of anticipation and leave fond memories—Pear Belle Helene, Banana Eclair and strudel made from dough so thin you can read through it.

Owner/chef Louis Szathmary is indeed a living legend. He was born in Hungary, earned a Ph.D. in psychology, and lived in Austria and other western European countries before coming to the U.S. in 1951. He worked as a chef in New England prior to joining Armour and Company in Chicago and, with his wife Sada, founded the Bakery in 1962.

2218 North Lincoln Avenue

## THE BAKERY

### STOCKYARD INN MARINATED BEEF

- 1 pound boiled, broiled or roasted beef, cut in julienne strips
- 1 large onion, julienned
- Juice of one lemon
- Salt, to taste
- 1½ tablespoons prepared mustard
- 2 tablespoons sugar
- ¼ teaspoon ground black pepper
- 2 teaspoons curry powder
- 2 cups sour cream
- ½ cup white vinegar
- Lettuce leaves, for decoration
- Sprinkling of paprika
- Chopped parsley, for decoration

1. In a large bowl, mix together the beef and onion. Sprinkle with lemon juice and salt. Let stand at room temperature for 20 minutes.
2. In another bowl, mix the mustard, sugar, pepper and curry until it forms a paste. Gently fold the sour cream and vinegar into the mixture. Fold this sauce into the beef and onions. Let it marinate in the refrigerator for at least 4 hours.
3. Taste for salt; add more if necessary. Serve on beds of lettuce leaves, sprinkle with paprika and parsley.

## The Bakery

### CAULIFLOWER SOUP

- 2 tablespoons shortening (preferably lard)
- ½ cup chopped onion
- 1 small carrot, scraped
- 1 cup chopped celery
- 1 tablespoon sugar
- 1 head firm white cauliflower, cut into small florets
- 2 tablespoons chopped fresh parsley
- 2 quarts veal or chicken stock or canned chicken broth diluted, to make 2 quarts
- ½ teaspoon peppercorns, ½ bay leaf, 1 teaspoon tarragon tied in a cheesecloth
- 1 tablespoon salt
- 4 tablespoons butter
- 6 tablespoons flour
- 2 cups milk
- 1 cup half and half
- 1 cup sour cream, room temperature

1. In a large soup pot, melt the shortening. Add the onion and cook over medium heat, stirring constantly, until onion starts to turn yellow. Add the carrot and celery and cook another 2 minutes. Add sugar, cauliflower and 1 tablespoon of the parsley. Cover and cook over very low heat, stirring occasionally to prevent sticking.
2. After 15 minutes add the stock of your choice and the cheesecloth bag of herbs and ½ tablespoon of salt. Bring to boil over medium heat. Reduce to a simmer.
3. In a small saucepan, melt the butter. Mix the flour into the milk with a wire whip. Stirring constantly with the whip, slowly add the flour-milk mixture into the butter. If added slowly enough thickening will occur immediately. Remove from heat and dilute with half and half.
4. Pour this mixture into the simmering soup. Stir gently and let simmer another 15 to 20 minutes. Check for taste and add more salt if necessary. (The saltiness of the stock used will make a difference.)

## The Bakery

5. Just before serving, place the sour cream in the soup tureen. Mix in the remaining parsley. Place two or three ladles of hot soup in the tureen and stir it into the sour cream. Remove the cheesecloth herb bag from the soup and add the remaining soup to the tureen. Serve immediately.

*If you make your own veal or chicken stock for this soup, be sure that the green leaves, white stalk and hard white core of the cauliflower are all cooked with the soup bones. The stock will take on a cauliflower taste. If you use canned chicken broth, chop the cauliflower trimmings and boil them in the water you use to dilute the canned broth.*

### BAKED GROUPER WITH SAUCE LOUIS AND HOT HERB BUTTER

4 tablespoons oil
3½ to 4 pounds grouper fillets
1 tablespoon CHEF'S SALT
1 teaspoon tarragon
1 teaspoon rosemary
½ teaspoon chervil
2 tablespoons butter
1 large bunch fresh parsley, for decoration
2 large lemons, cut into wedges
1 recipe HOT HERB BUTTER

1. Preheat oven to 375°. Cover the rack of a broiler pan with aluminum foil. Brush 2 tablespoons of oil on the foil.
2. Rub both sides of the fish with Chef's Salt. Mix tarragon, rosemary and chervil in a small bowl with the butter. Add 2 tablespoons of oil. Spread this mixture on the flesh side of the fillets and place them, skin side down on the foil. With a small knife, gently make two or three lengthwise cuts into the fish, being careful not to go deeper than half the thickness of the fillet. Then cut six or eight times crosswise. Bake for about 20 minutes.
3. Check doneness by inserting two forks in the thickest part of the fillet and pulling apart slightly. If it flakes and is not translucent, the fish is done.
4. Remove to a large serving platter. Surround with fresh parsley and lemon wedges. Serve with Hot Herb Butter and Sauce Louis.

# The Bakery

## CHEF'S SALT

1 cup salt
1 tablespoon Spanish or Hungarian paprika
1 teaspoon freshly ground black pepper
¼ teaspoon ground white pepper
¼ teaspoon garlic salt

Mix well and store in a covered jar until ready for use.

## HOT HERB BUTTER

1 cup butter
1 lemon
1 teaspoon tarragon
1 teaspoon rosemary
1 teaspoon basil
4 or 5 sprigs fresh parsley, dried
2 to 4 tablespoons brandy or cognac

1. Heat butter in a small saucepan. With a zester or grater, scrape about ½ teaspoon of lemon zest into the butter.
2. Cut the lemon, squeeze juice through a sieve into a cup. Put 1 tablespoon water in each lemon half; stir it with a spoon to scrape off all the flesh of the lemon. Press through a sieve.
3. Add tarragon, rosemary and basil to the lemon juice. Stir into the butter. Keep this herb butter warm.
4. Dip the dried parsley sprigs into the brandy or cognac and place on the fish. Heat the remaining cognac, pour over the fish and ignite. The cognac-dipped herbs will burn to ash. When the flame has died out, spoon the Hot Herb Butter over the fish.

# The Bakery

### SAUCE LOUIS

2 eggs
3 tablespoons prepared mustard
3 tablespoons sugar
½ teaspoon salt
⅛ teaspoon white pepper
Juice of one lemon
1 teaspoon vinegar
2 cups sour cream

1. In a medium-size bowl, blend together the eggs, mustard, sugar, salt, pepper, lemon juice and vinegar with a wire whip.
2. Slowly fold in the sour cream. Refrigerate until ready to use with fish or cold meats. Makes 2½ cups.

### CELERY KNOB REMOULADE

3 to 4 large celery knobs (celeriac), about 2–2½ lbs. total
1 teaspoon salt
⅔ cups vinegar
3 tablespoons Dijon-style mustard
Salt, to taste
¼ teaspoon white pepper
⅔ cup oil
Juice of ½ lemon
2 to 3 tablespoons freshly chopped parsley

1. Peel the celery knobs and cut them into thin julienne strips. Sprinkle the strips with salt and vinegar and let stand 15 minutes. Drain.
2. Blend together the mustard, a little salt and white pepper. Using a wire whip, gradually beat in the oil. Add the lemon juice.
3. Toss the celery with the remoulade sauce and place it in a serving dish. Sprinkle the top with the parsley.

*If you want your celery remoulade to be snow white, while you are cutting the julienne strips have a plastic bowl with enough cold water mixed with vinegar to cover the julienne strips. Keep the peeled uncut celery and the strips in the vinegar water until you start to make the salad.*

## The Bakery

### BROWNIE BOTTOM BOURBON PIE

- 5 egg yolks
- ¾ cup sugar
- 1 envelope unflavored gelatin
- ¼ cup cold water
- ½ cup bourbon
- 3 cups heavy cream
- Pinch of salt
- Pinch of sugar
- 1 10" brownie, baked from your own recipe

1. Beat the egg yolks until thick and lemon-colored. Slowly beat in the sugar.
2. Soften the gelatin in the cold water and add one-third of the bourbon. Heat over boiling water until the gelatin dissolves. Add this to the yolks and stir briskly. Stir in the remaining bourbon. Whip 1 cup heavy cream and fold into the mixture.
3. Pour the filling into the pan containing the brownie and chill at least 4 hours.
4. Top the pie with the remaining heavy cream whipped with a few grains of salt and just a pinch of sugar. If you wish, sprinkle about 2 tablespoons shaved chocolate on top.

*After you have made this dish once or twice, you may find you wish to use more sugar in the heavy cream or less bourbon in the filling. If you cut down on the bourbon, be sure to make up the difference in quantity with cold water.*

## THE BAKERY

### CHOCOLATE SAUCE

¼ cup unsalted butter
1 cup sugar
½ cup good quality cocoa
1 cup milk

1 tablespoon cornstarch
¼ cup cold water
½ cup chocolate syrup
    (preferably Hershey's)
¼ cup brandy

1. In a very heavy saucepan, melt the butter with the sugar and cocoa until the mixture starts to caramelize. Immediately add the milk, stirring constantly. The hard lumps will dissolve as the liquid comes to a boil.
2. Dilute the cornstarch with the water. Pour this in a slow stream into the boiling syrup, stirring constantly.
3. Remove from the heat and cool to room temperature.
4. Add the chocolate syrup and brandy. Refrigerate. Makes about 2 cups.

*The saucepan must be very heavy in order to melt the butter and chocolate with the sugar until the sugar begins to carmelize. This mixture not only browns but begins to harden. The carmelized sugar will "toast" the cocoa somewhat, and the butter will get a burned taste. These are the secret flavor components of the sauce. Recipe may be doubled or quadrupled, but it will take longer.*

# Cape Cod Room

*Dinner for Six*

*Salad of Sea Scallops and Shrimp with Basil Viniagrette*

*Boston Clam Chowder*

*Coleslaw*

*Lobster à la Newburg*

*Rice Pudding*

*The Drake Hotel, Owner*

# Cape Cod Room

The Drake Hotel was proclaimed an historic landmark by the United States Department of the Interior and the State of Illinois. It is in the National Register of Historic Places. Outside, the thirteen-story classical façade of the Drake is of solid Bedford limestone. Inside, its floors are of Tennessee marble. The New England style, complete with its collection of old glass bottles, exposed wood beams, copper pots and lobster shells, evokes thoughts of distant harbors and rocky shores.

The charming ambiance is only enhanced by the equally charming manager Patrick Bredin. He sets the congenial tone of the restaurant. He is proud of the famous and near-famous guests he has greeted over the years. "I remember when Governor Reagan sat over there or when Mickey Rooney sat here," Bredin smiles "My goal is to have our guests happy," he continues. Chef Leo Waldmeier agrees: "I firmly believe that a chef never stops learning and that eating should be a total experience which melds food and atmosphere to an essence of one."

For the oyster lover the Oyster Festival boasts Belon, Chatham, Orleans and Cockenoes in a variety of styles. All in all, the Cape Cod Room remains one of the best sources of dependably excellent food.

The Drake Hotel, Michigan Avenue and Walton Street

## Cape Cod Room

### SALAD OF SEA SCALLOPS AND SHRIMP WITH BASIL VINAIGRETTE

- 4 cups water
- 1 cup dry white wine
- 8 to 10 peppercorns crushed
- ½ teaspoon thyme
- 1 bay leaf
- 2 tablespoons finely chopped onion
- 2 tablespoons finely chopped carrot
- 8 large shrimp, peeled, deveined and halved lengthwise
- 10 sea scallops, halved
- ½ fresh cucumber, peeled and seeded
- 1 firm tomato, peeled and seeded
- 8 medium-size fresh mushrooms
- 1 small leek, white only
- BASIL VINAIGRETTE
- Walnuts

1. Place water and wine in a 4-quart stock pot over medium-high heat and bring to a boil. Add the peppercorns, thyme, bay leaf, onion and carrot. Simmer for 10 minutes. Season to taste.
2. Add shrimp and scallops. Simmer 2 minutes. Then remove seafood with slotted spoon and keep fresh in lukewarm water that barely covers.
3. Cut cucumber, tomato, mushrooms and leek in very fine strips. Arrange attractively on a plate and decorate with drained seafood.
4. Sprinkle lightly with Basil Vinaigrette and garnish with walnuts.

### BASIL VINAIGRETTE

- ¼ cup walnut oil
- 2 to 3 tablespoons sherry vinegar
- 1 tablespoon finely chopped shallot
- 1 tablespoon finely chopped basil
- Salt and freshly ground black pepper
- 2 tablespoon finely chopped walnuts

Place walnut oil, vinegar, shallot, basil, salt and pepper in a small bowl and combine with a whisk.

## Cape Cod Room

### BOSTON CLAM CHOWDER

12 fresh large clams
2 quarts water
1 pound potatoes, diced, peeled
½ green pepper, diced
3 ribs celery, sliced
1 teaspoon flour dissolved in 1 tablespoon water
1 teaspoon salt
½ teaspoon Worcestershire sauce
1 (3 ounce) can chopped clams
1 cup cream

1. Cook fresh clams in water for 10 minutes. Drain.
2. Add potatoes, green pepper and celery; simmer for 1 hour.
3. Combine flour and water in ¼ cup of the chowder. Add mixture back to the chowder, stirring constantly, to thicken.
4. Add salt, Worcestershire sauce and canned clams; simmer for 15 minutes. Remove from heat. Mix in cream. Serve hot.

*Bostonians would use available fish in their chowders. Spices and herbs would be added according to taste. In the New York area tomatoes are combined with the clams and called Manhattan clam chowder. Bostonians frown on this innovation.*

# Cape Cod Room

Note: All entrees at the Cape Cod Room are served with au gratin potatoes, a choice of mixed green salad or this special creamy coleslaw.

## COLESLAW

- 2 tablespoons cider vinegar
- 2 tablespoons oil
- 2 cups finely shredded cabbage
- ⅓ cup sour cream
- ⅓ cup mayonnaise
- ¾ teaspoon salt
- ¼ teaspoon pepper

1. Combine cider vinegar and oil in a small mixing bowl.
2. Place cabbage in a large mixing bowl, suitable for serving.
3. Toss cabbage with vinegar-oil mixture.
4. Blend together sour cream, mayonnaise, salt and pepper.
5. Toss sour cream mixture with cabbage. Cover and chill overnight.

## Cape Cod Room

### LOBSTER à la NEWBURG

- ¼ pound butter
- 1 pound Maine lobster meat, cooked, diced
- ½ teaspoon paprika
- 1 tablespoon flour
- 4 teaspoons sherry, pale dry or Amontillado
- 1¼ cups heavy cream
- 4 egg yolks, slightly beaten
- Salt and pepper to taste
- Buttered toast points

1. Melt butter slowly in a large heavy skillet. Lightly sauté lobster meat.
2. Add paprika, stir until smooth. Sprinkle flour over lobster, stir, mix well.
3. Mix in Sherry.
4. Add cream, allow mixture to come to a boil. Reduce heat, add beaten egg yolks slowly, stirring until mixture is combined and is desired thickness. Do not overcook. Serve over buttered toast points.

*Lutz Olkiewicz, The Drake Hotel's head pastry chef, is a master of his craft, always approaching his work with an artist's eye. Olkiewicz began as an apprentice at age seven in his aunt's pastry and tea shop in his hometown of Kolber, Germany. Lutz's awards are many. His creations vary from paper-thin yeast dough flowers to cathedrals made with sugar cubes and landscape paintings formed with cocoa. It is Olkiewicz's demand for perfection and his ability that has brought him wide acclaim.*

# Cape Cod Room

## RICE PUDDING

1 cup rice
1 pint milk
3 cups half and half
½ cup sugar

Pinch of salt
1 teaspoon vanilla
LIQUID EGG CUSTARD
1 cup golden raisins

1. Preheat oven to 375°.
2. Steam rice in milk and half and half in top of double boiler over warm, but not boiling water. Remove from stove and mix in sugar, salt, vanilla and Egg Custard.
3. Spread raisins over bottom of 2½-quart oven-baking casserole. Add pudding mixture. Place a large pan in oven and arrange casserole in pan. Fill pan two-thirds way with hot water. Bake for 45 minutes to one hour. Cool to room temperature; refrigerate until ready to serve.

Note: Custard should be soft when removed from oven. It will set up during cooling.

## LIQUID EGG CUSTARD

2 cups milk
5 eggs
½ cup sugar
1 cup half and half

⅛ teaspoon salt
Vanilla, to taste
3 drops yellow food coloring

Mix all ingredients in a large bowl with a wire whisk. Pour mixture through a strainer. Cover and refrigerate any leftover custard for future recipes.

*Dinner for Six*

*Shrimp and Crabmeat Salad*

*Fried Calamari*

*Cioppino*

*Crème Brûllé*

*Wine:*

*With Appetizers: Girard Dry Chenin Blanc*
*or*
*St. Francis Gewürztraminer*

*With Cioppino: Ridge Zinfandel*
*or*
*Jordan Cabernet Sauvignon*

*David Hoemann, General Manager*

*Barry Brooks, Corporate Chef*

## Chestnut Street Grill

Turn of the century Chicago architecture and fine interiors by designer Miesel are handsomely integrated at the Chestnut Street Grill. The classic atmosphere is maintained with fresh flowers on every table, lamps from an old school house in St. Louis, tile floors and a circular bar.

The centrally displayed kitchen highlights the grill where Mexican mesquite and charcoals work their magic on fresh seafood. "Our restaurant is popular because of the way we prepare the food. It is cooked simply over a charcoal grill. We basically don't use sauces, maybe just a topping or a bit of drawn butter. You can't hide the quality of food if you do not use sauces. This food styling is for the society that is diet and/or health conscious," says David Hoemann.

Entrees include grilled steak, calves liver with onions, calamari, and swordfish steak. The Chestnut Street Grill is famous for its delicious cappucino ice cream, flown in from Los Angeles.

Hoemann adds, "The new American cuisine is truly exciting, not overdone, just right."

Water Tower Place, Michigan Avenue

## Chestnut Street Grill

### SHRIMP AND CRABMEAT SALAD

| | |
|---|---|
| 12 ounces baby Alaskan shrimp | 1 large head Romaine lettuce |
| 10 ounces Alaskan king crabmeat | 1 large head Boston lettuce |
| | 2 large tomatoes |

1. Wash lettuce in cold water; separate leaves; pat dry. Tear leaves into smaller pieces.
2. Cut each tomato into six wedges. Toss with lettuce in large bowl.
3. Sprinkle top of salad with the shrimp and crabmeat. Serve with Tomato Dressing.

### TOMATO DRESSING

| | |
|---|---|
| 3 plum tomatoes, seeded, quartered | 2 tablespoons chopped chives |
| ¾ cup mayonnaise | Salt and pepper, to taste |
| ¾ cup sour cream | ¼ teaspoon sugar |
| | 2 to 3 tablespoons milk |

1. Insert steel blade in bowl of food processor. Process tomatoes slightly, leaving them in small pieces.
2. Add remaining ingredients, blend quickly.
3. Store tomato dressing in covered container in refrigerator.

## Chestnut Street Grill

### FRIED CALAMARI

*2 pounds squid*  
*3 cups vegetable oil*  
*Flour*  
*Salt, to taste*  
*6 lemon wedges*

1. Clean squid (see note). Cut into ½-inch circles.
2. Heat oil in fryer, large heavy pot, or wok to 375°. Roll squid in flour. Shake off excess so that just a light coating remains.
3. Carefully slide squid pieces into hot oil for approximately 3 to 5 minutes. Cook one-third of the squid at a time. (This prevents the temperature of the oil from dropping too much.)
4. Remove squid from oil and place on paper towels to drain.
5. Sprinkle with salt and lemon juice. Serve immediately.

*If cleaned squid are not available from your fishmonger, you can clean them yourselves by following these steps:*
1. *Hold main body and gently pull tentacles from out body sac.*
2. *Remove the thin shell from inside. Grab the shell (protruding bone) with thumb and pull to separate.*
3. *Hold squid under running water and pull away outer membrane.*
4. *Turn body sac inside out and rinse well.*
5. *Cut below eye to remove tentacles and fry whole.*

## Chestnut Street Grill

### CIOPPINO

18 Littleneck clams
24 farm mussels
12 (16–20 count size) shrimp
24 ounces whitefish, any kind, boned
12 ounces Alaskan king crablegs
12 ounces sea scallops
3 quarts CIOPPINO SAUCE

1. Preheat oven to 350°.
2. Wash clams, mussels and shrimp. Place all seafood into a large ovenproof pot.
3. Pour Cioppino Sauce over the seafood. Bake at 350° for about 45 minutes. Clams and mussels must all open. Discard those that don't.
4. Serve in warm soup dishes.

## Chestnut Street Grill

### CIOPPINO SAUCE

- ⅓ cup oil
- 1 tablespoon chopped garlic
- 1 large onion, diced
- 1 large green pepper, diced
- 2 stalks celery, diced
- 2 tablespoons oregano
- 2 tablespoons basil
- 1 tablespoon black pepper
- 48 ounces canned whole tomatoes
- 24 ounces tomato puree
- ⅓ cup white wine
- 1 teaspoon Tabasco sauce
- 2 tablespoons salt
- 3 tablespoons sugar

1. Lightly brown oil and garlic in a large saucepan. Add onions. Cook until tender over medium heat, stirring occasionally. Add oregano, basil and pepper to the onion mixture. Cook for 1 minute.
2. While onions are cooking, sauté green pepper and celery in another skillet.
3. Add green pepper and celery to onions. Puree tomatoes in blender and add to onions and spices. Stir in tomato puree. Rinse tomato puree can with water leaving about half of the can filled. Add to sauce.
4. Pour in wine and Tabasco sauce. Simmer for 1½ hours.
5. Add salt and sugar. Continue cooking for an additional ½ hour on low heat.

*It is said that this tomato-based shellfish stew originated in San Francisco. Be sure to serve lots of sourdough bread with your Cioppino.*

# Chestnut Street Grill

## CRÊME BRÛLEÉ

5 egg yolks
½ cup sugar
2 cups heavy cream
2 tablespoons vanilla

Boiling water
4 tablespoons brown sugar, sifted

1. Preheat oven to 325°. Beat egg yolks and sugar at high speed until light and fluffy.
2. Heat cream to lukewarm in a heavy saucepan. Combine egg mixture and cream. Do not beat. Add vanilla.
3. Pour mixture into ovenproof, 6-ounce ramakins. Fill to the rim.
4. Place ramakins into a roasting pan. Pour boiling water into the roasting pan until it reaches middle of the ramakins. Cook for 45 minutes or until inserted knife comes out clean. Remove ramakins from pan, cool and refrigerate.
5. Place ramakins in roasting pan of ice. Sprinkle tops with brown sugar. Place under broiler and broil about 15 to 30 seconds until sugar caramelizes. Serve immediately.

*Dinner for Six*

*Champignons Farcis (Stuffed Mushrooms)*

*Chez Paul Salad*

*Consommé Chantilly or Milanaise*

*Salmon en Croûte*

*Strawberries Romanoff*

*Wine:*

*Pinot Noir, Clos du Bois 1978*

*Bill Contos, Owner*

*George Hamilton, Chef*

# CHEZ PAUL

Chez Paul is as popular today as it was 37 years ago when its doors first opened for business. It is situated in a stately, old, corner yellow brick mansion townhouse, dating from the late 19th century. Chez Paul has a warmth and personality all its own. A doorman is on hand to assist you upon entering. Inside are painted steel gray walls, black leather seats, individual rooms and draperies in a warm deep red tapestry. The walls are resplendent with oil paintings and crystal chandeliers sparkle from the ceiling. Warmth and elegance envelop you.

Owner Bill Contos is rightly proud of the fact that Chez Paul was opened by his parents and that the restaurant is the oldest family operated restaurant in the greater Chicago area. In 1945 Bill's father, referred to fondly as Papa, Paul himself and his mother worked together to lay the foundation for this fine restaurant. "It was different then; people didn't go out for dinner as they do now," says Bill. "Mother was the cashier. It was a lot of work then." After a stint in the army Bill joined the family business by starting in the kitchen.

The Chez Paul reputation has been secured by a very loyal clientele over the years. For as Bill says, "Food should be personalized; it should be served and prepared with love. The food business in general is with love."

660 North Rush Street

# Chez Paul

## CHAMPIGNONS FARCIS (STUFFED MUSHROOMS)

1 pound large mushrooms
3 tablespoons olive oil
Salt and white pepper, to taste
½ pound tenderloin, ground
4 shallots, minced
1 onion, minced
1 tablespoon brandy
¼ pound Swiss cheese slices, cut into 1" squares
BORDELAISE SAUCE

1. Clean mushrooms; remove stems.
2. Heat 2 tablespoons oil in a large heavy skillet. Sauté mushrooms lightly. Season with salt and pepper to taste. Drain mushrooms on paper towels.
3. Combine ground tenderloin, shallots, onions and brandy in a mixing bowl. Sauté mixture in remaining olive oil until meat is cooked. Stir occasionally. Cool to room temperature.
4. Stuff mushrooms with tenderloin mixture. Place a piece of Swiss cheese over each mushroom. Arrange mushrooms on a cookie sheet. Broil 1 minute or until cheese melts.
5. Place mushrooms on individual plates. Serve with Bordelaise Sauce.

## Chez Paul

### BORDELAISE SAUCE

2 tablespoons butter
3 shallots, minced
⅔ cup red wine
1⅓ cup BROWN SAUCE
2 tablespoons lemon juice
Salt and pepper, to taste

1. Heat butter in heavy saucepan and sauté minced shallots until soft. Add the red wine. Reduce. Add Brown Sauce and reduce again by half.
2. Mix in lemon juice; season with salt and pepper to taste. Makes about 1½ cups of Sauce.

### BROWN SAUCE

¼ pound butter
½ cup flour
1 quart beef stock
1 cup red wine
¼ cup tomato puree
Salt and pepper, to taste

1. Melt the butter in a heavy skillet over medium heat. Whisk in the flour, continuing to cook for 5 to 6 minutes. Stir constantly.
2. Heat the beef stock in a deep 2- to 3-quart saucepan. Whisk in half of the flour roux.
3. Whisk in the remaining roux, the wine and tomato puree. Season with salt and pepper. Bring mixture to a boil, reduce heat and simmer for 1 hour.
4. Cool and strain, then refrigerate or freeze.

*Use the finest white, firm mushrooms you can find. If you prefer, the mushrooms can be blanched instead of sautéed.*

*Brown Sauce is a versatile foundation in cooking. It freezes well, hence defrost when needed.*

# Chez Paul

## CHEZ PAUL SALAD

- 4 medium-size heads Bibb lettuce
- 3 large tomatoes, sliced
- 1 (14-ounce) can hearts of palm, drained, sliced
- 2 avocados, peeled, pitted, sliced
- CHEZ PAUL DRESSING

1. Clean and wash the lettuce. Pat dry. Gently tear lettuce away from the core.
2. Arrange the lettuce, tomatoes, hearts of palm and avocados on chilled salad plates.
3. Drizzle dressing over salad.

### CHEZ PAUL DRESSING

- ¾ cup olive oil
- ¼ cup red wine vinegar
- 1 teaspoon Dijon mustard
- ½ teaspoon salt
- ½ teaspoon ground black pepper

Combine all ingredients in a jar. Shake vigorously. Refrigerate until ready for use.

# CHEZ PAUL

## CONSOMMÉ CHANTILLY or MILANAISE

- 1 pound beef bones and shanks, cracked
- 2 carrots, coarsely chopped
- 1 leek, cut into 2" pieces
- 1 rib celery, coarsely chopped
- 1 teaspoon fennel
- 1 teaspoon salt
- 1 teaspoon pepper
- BOUQUET GARNI
- 5 eggs, separated, reserve shells
- 1 cup heavy cream
- 3 teaspoons chopped chives
- 3 sprigs parsley, chopped

1. Place beef bones, carrots, leek, celery, fennel, salt, pepper and Bouquet Garni in a large stock pot. Cover with cold water. Bring to a boil. Reduce heat and simmer uncovered for 5 to 6 hours. Remove any scum as it may form on the top.
2. Bring Consommé to a boil, add slightly beaten egg whites and egg shells. Continue cooking until the egg whites have risen to the surface, about 15 minutes. Do not stir or boil. Remove from heat, cool. Strain with a double layer of cheesecloth.
3. Combine egg yolks and cream. Add egg yolk mixture to Consommé in a slow steady stream.
4. Remove shells. Ladle in heated soup cups. Garnish with chives and parsley.

*The egg whites and egg shells are used as a clarifying agent in the Consummé. Prepare Consummé the day before you plan to serve.*

# Chez Paul

## SALMON en CROÛTE with SAUCE à l'OSEILLE

3½ to 4 pounds salmon, boned, skinned, cut into 2 filets
½ pound fresh sorrel or spinach, stems removed
¼ cup parsley, chopped
¼ cup chopped onions
5 hard-boiled eggs, shelled
Salt and pepper, to taste
PUFF PASTRY
1 lemon, sliced
SAUCE à l'OSEILLE

1. Preheat oven to 375°.
2. Place one fillet of salmon on a cold flat surface. Shred sorrel and arrange over salmon. Combine parsley, onion and chopped eggs. Spread mixture evenly over the sorrel. Sprinkle with salt and pepper. Cover with other fillet of salmon.
3. Roll out puff pastry. Place salmon in center of pastry. Fold pastry over salmon and seal by firmly pressing edges together.
4. Line baking sheet with parchment paper. Place salmon on baking sheet. Make ½-inch steam vent in pastry. Bake for 45 to 60 minutes or until golden brown. Garnish with lemon slices and serve with warm Sauce à l'Oseille.

*Sorrel is mentioned as early as the 13th century. It is used as a base for soups and sauces.*

### PUFF PASTRY

4 cups flour
1 teaspoon salt
2 cups butter, chilled in ½" pieces
1 cup water

1. Place flour and salt in a large mixing bowl. Combine with bits of butter, using fingertips. Gradually stir in the water making a firm sticky dough. Chill dough for 15 minutes.
2. Roll out dough on a lightly floured surface into a rectangle 14 inches by 18 inches. Fold dough over in an envelope style. Cover with plastic wrap and chill for 45 minutes. Repeat three more times.
3. Roll dough out to a ⅛-inch thickness. Proceed with use in recipe.

*Scraps of puff pastry that are left over can be rerolled and frozen or perhaps cut into crescent shapes for garnish.*

# Chez Paul

## SAUCE à l'OSEILLE

- 4 shallots
- ¼ cup FISH STOCK
- 1½ cup dry vermouth
- 1 cup dry white wine
- 2 cups cream
- Salt and pepper, to taste
- ½ pound sorrel, stems removed
- 3 egg yolks
- ¼ cup cream
- 1 tablespoon lemon juice

1. Combine shallots, Fish Stock, dry vermouth, and white wine in a deep heavy skillet. Cook over high heat for 45 minutes or until liquid is reduced to about half a cup.
2. Add 2 cups of cream, salt and pepper to taste. Bring mixture to a boil. Cook over high heat for 10 minutes.
3. Cut the sorrel into very fine shreds. Add sorrel to liquid and bring to a boil. Beat egg yolks with ¼-cup cream. Remove sauce from the heat, stir in the yolk and cream. Season with lemon juice and salt and pepper.
4. Keep the sauce warm but do not bring to a boil or it will curdle.

*Spinach may be substituted for the sorrel.*

## FISH STOCK

- 1 quart water
- 1 medium onion, sliced
- 2 ribs celery, sliced
- 1 pound bones, head and skin of a fish
- 3 black peppercorns
- 1 large bay leaf

Place all ingredients in a large pot. Cover with water. Simmer for approximately 45 to 60 minutes. Strain through cheesecloth. Makes 1 quart of stock.

## Chez Paul

**STRAWBERRIES ROMANOFF**

1 quart strawberries
2 cups port
French vanilla ice cream
½ pint heavy cream
4 tablespoons sugar
Grand Marnier or other orange-flavored liqueur

1. Wash and hull strawberries and slice. Place in a serving bowl, toss with port and allow to marinate 30 minutes.
2. Place a scoop of vanilla ice cream in each of 6 dessert bowls.
3. Arrange strawberries over the ice cream.
4. Whip cream in a chilled bowl on high speed. Gradually add sugar. Continue beating until cream is stiff. Chill until ready to use.
5. Places dollops of whipped cream around ice cream. Drizzle with Grand Marnier.

# ·THE·CONSORT·

*Dinner for Four*

*Salmon Finger Tips with Pine Nuts and Basil Sauce*

*Butter Lettuce with Carrot Strings with
Goat Cheese and Yogurt Cream Dressing*

*Roast Duck with Fresh Melon*

*Linzertorte*

*Wine:*

*Fleurie 1981*

*Westin Hotel, Owner*

*Vlastimil Lebeda, Executive Chef*

## The Consort

Executive Chef Vlastimil Lebeda oversees the massive operation of the food service at the Westin Hotel on Michigan Avenue. A few months after the Soviet army invaded Czechoslovakia in the fall of 1968, Lebeda left Liberec for a visit with friends in Germany. He had told the hotel that he would be gone four days. Packing a single suitcase he drove to Munich. Five days later, he boarded a plane for Canada. Lebeda began working in Regina, Saskatchewan. From Canada and an association with the Westin Hotels he moved to his present position in Chicago.

At the Consort, he combines his stylish American cuisine with a decor of live greenery, beveled mirrors, plush silver, gold and amethyst upholstery and outstanding service to create a truly memorable culinary event.

Westin Hotel, 909 North Michigan Avenue

## THE CONSORT

### SALMON FINGER TIPS WITH PINE NUTS AND BASIL SAUCE

1 pound fresh salmon fillet, boneless and skinless
Salt and white pepper, to taste
3 tablespoons butter
3 ounces white vermouth
1½ cups heavy cream
5 sprigs fresh basil, chopped finely
1½ ounces pine nuts, roasted

1. Cut salmon in strips, finger shaped, approximately 1 ounce each.
2. Season with salt and pepper.
3. Melt butter in skillet; when hot, sauté fingers to medium done.
4. Remove salmon and keep warm.
5. Strain fat from skillet and deglaze with vermouth.
6. Add heavy cream and reduce it by half over moderate heat.
7. Mix in chopped basil and season with salt and pepper.
8. Spoon approximately 2 ounces of sauce on plates, place 3 salmon fingers atop sauce on each plate. Sprinkle with pine nuts; garnish with basil leaves and serve.

### BUTTERLEAF LETTUCE WITH CARROT STRINGS

2 small heads Butterleaf lettuce
2 ounces fresh carrots, cut in julienne strings

GOAT CHEESE AND YOGURT CREAM DRESSING

1. Wash lettuce and arrange on plates. Garnish lettuce with carrots.
2. Drizzle dressing over salad.

# THE CONSORT

## GOAT CHEESE AND YOGURT DRESSING

1 cup plain yogurt
5 ounces goat cheese
   (Montrachet is also
   suitable)

2 ounces heavy cream
Salt and pepper, to taste

1. Mix yogurt and goat cheese in blender or food processor fitted with steel blade.
2. Add heavy cream; blend.
3. Season with salt and pepper. If dressing is too thick add milk.

*Goat cheese dressing should be served at room temperature.*

## ROAST DUCK WITH FRESH MELON

2 ducklings, 4 pounds each
   Salt
1½ medium-size canteloupes,
   ripe
½ medium-size honeydew
   melon, ripe

3 ounces Midori melon
   liqueur
Pinch cayenne pepper
Pinch English mustard
1 tablespoon butter

1. Preheat oven to 350°.
2. Sprinkle ducks with salt, place in roasting pan and roast in oven until done and skin is nice and crisp. Baste ducks during roasting with drippings. Remove and keep warm.
3. Cut melons in half, remove seeds and make 12 melon balls from each. Remove rest of the flesh from each melon and place in a food procesor fitted with steel blade or blender and blend well.
4. Strain all fat from roasting pan and deglaze with Midori liqueur. Add puree of melons and simmer until sauce thickens. Season with cayenne, mustard and salt to taste.
5. Sauté melon balls in pan with butter, just to make them warm.
6. Debone ducks, place on plates, pour on sauce and garnish with melon balls.

## The Consort

### LINZERTORTE

- 4 cups flour
- 10 ounces butter
- 1½ cups sugar
- 3 eggs
- 9 ounces hazelnuts, finely grated
- ⅛ teaspoon cinnamon
- ¼ ounce salt
- 1 tablespoon rum
- Milk, as needed
- Raspberry jam, about 1 pound
- Confectioner's sugar

1. Preheat oven to 400°.
2. Put flour on a board or in a large bowl and make a well in the center. Place butter, sugar and eggs in the well and blend.
3. Gradually mix the grated nuts, cinnamon and salt into the flour mixture.
4. Milk is added as needed until the ingredients form a stiff dough. Allow dough to rest 1 hour in a cool place.
5. Roll dough out to a ¼-inch thickness. Line the bottoms of spring form pans with the dough.
6. Fill the center with raspberry jam and arrange thin strips of the dough in a lattice pattern over the jam.
7. Bake at 400° for 20 to 25 minutes.
8. When the torte has cooled, remove it from the pan and sprinkle with confectioner's sugar.

*This recipe makes three Linzertortes. They freeze well. This is the famous torte from Linz, Austria. It is my husband's favorite.—B.G.*

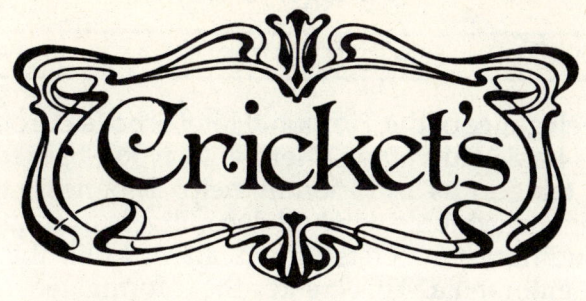

*Dinner for Six*

*Linguini Primavera Salad*

*Senegalaise Soup*

*Veal Cricket's*

*Hot Cabbage à la Reims*

*Roast Goat Cheese*

*Chocolate Cake sans Farine*

*Wine:*

*Salad and Soup, 1980 Johanisberger Klaus Riesling Kabinett*

*Veal, 1977 Chambolle Musigny, Ropiteau*

*Dessert, 1978 Chateau de Suduiraut*

*John Lever, Manager*

## CRICKET'S

The quiet elegance of the Tremont Hotel echoes European quality. Cricket's has a club atmosphere with wood-backed chairs, red checked tablecloths and friendly help. Enhancing the room are logos and corporate symbols perched decoratively from the low ceiling and walls including local TV stations, Standard Oil, the Blackhawks and Chicago memorabilia. This creates the informal feel of the restaurant. "People come here to Cricket's for the good food and atmosphere," says manager John Lever. "The majority of our clientele are regulars," he continues. "We are built on Chicago business."

The extensive menu offers continental cuisine with beautiful detail given to each dish: Terrine de Canard en Gelee; Creme Senegalaise Soup; Rabbit with Leeks and Thyme; Roast Duckling with Mangos. Grilled selections, fine desserts and a wide choice of wine round out a full menu. For a special treat, try the New Orleans brunch on Saturday and Sunday featuring Creole-style dishes with wonderful, spicy sauces.

Cricket's is a recipient of the Mobile Guide 4 Star award in 1983 and of Holiday Magazine awards.

100 East Chestnut

## CRICKET'S

### LINGUINI PRIMAVERA SALAD

1 cup broccoli florets
½ pound fresh green peas, shelled
½ pound green beans, cut
1 cup sliced carrots
1 cup sliced turnips
1 cup cauliflower florets
2 dozen asparagus tips
5 tomatoes, peeled, seeded, diced
1 cup mushroom caps, sliced
½ pound white linguini
½ pound green linguini
PESTO DRESSING
⅓ cup pine nuts
6 sprigs parsley
Parmesan cheese

1. Place broccoli florets in a saucepan of boiling water, reduce heat to a simmer and cook for 3 minutes. Drain, plunge into cold water and drain again. Repeat procedure with peas, beans, carrots, turnips, cauliflower and asparagus. Check carefully as each vegetable has its own cooking time. When done, place all vegetables in a large bowl. Mix with tomatoes and mushrooms and chill.
2. Cook pasta until al dente; drain. Place in cold water while preparing pesto.
3. Slowly toss drained linguini with vegetables and Pesto Dressing.
4. Divide onto six plates. Decorate with 1 broccoli, 1 cauliflower, 1 green bean and 2 asparagus tips on side of each plate.
5. Garnish with parsley. Serve with Parmesan cheese. Serve cold.

## CRICKET'S

### PESTO DRESSING

- ½ cup minced shallots
- ½ cup minced onion
- 2 teaspoons minced garlic
- 1 teaspoon anchovies
- 1 cup fresh basil leaves
- 1 teaspoon fresh tarragon leaves
- 2 teaspoons parsley
- 1 tablespoon fresh oregano
- 1 tablespoon fresh sage
- 1 tablespoon fresh chives
- 6 teaspoons pure olive oil
- Juice of one lemon
- Salt and pepper, to taste

1. Insert steel blade in food processor. Puree all the ingredients except olive oil, lemon juice and salt and pepper.
2. Add olive oil and lemon juice in a slow steady stream with the machine running. Season with salt and pepper. Refrigerate until ready to use.

*The white and green pasta is as delightful on the palate as to the eye. Pasta comes in an astonishing variety of designs and sizes. Try different ones.*

### SENEGALAISE SOUP

- 5 tablespoons butter
- 1 small onion, coarsely chopped
- 1 carrot, coarsely chopped
- 1 stalk celery, coarsely chopped
- 1 heaping teaspoon curry powder
- 3 small cinnamon sticks
- 2 bay leaves
- 1 teaspoon whole cloves
- 5 cups strong CHICKEN BROTH
- 1 tablespoon tomato puree
- 2 heaping tablespoons almond paste
- 1 tablespoon red currant jelly
- 3 tablespoons flour
- Salt and white pepper
- 1 pint heavy cream
- Toasted coconut, for garnish

## CRICKET'S

1. Melt 2 tablespoons butter in a large heavy saucepan over medium heat. Add onion, carrot and celery and stir until vegetables have taken on a little color.
2. Stir in curry powder. Add cinnamon sticks, bay leaves, cloves, chicken broth, tomato puree, almond paste and jelly. Mix well and bring to a boil. Reduce heat to simmer and continue cooking 1 hour. Skim off any foam that rises to the surface.
3. Heat remaining butter in a small skillet. Whisk together with the flour and simmer for 5 minutes, stirring with a wooden spoon. Slowly add the mixture to the soup, stirring until blended. Cool for 5 minutes or until slightly thickened.
4. Strain the soup. Adjust for seasonings, cool and refrigerate.
5. When ready to serve, combine with the cream. Sprinkle with coconuts.

### CHICKEN BROTH

| | |
|---|---|
| 2 pounds chicken parts, including skin | 3 stalks celery, including tops |
| 4 sprigs parsley | 1 large onion, sliced |
| 1 large carrot, roughly chopped | 1 teaspoon salt |
| | ½ teaspoon pepper |

1. Cover ingredients with cold water in a large stock pot. Bring to a boil. Reduce to a simmer, cover and cook for 2 hours. Skim off the surface occasionally.
2. Strain broth; chill in refrigerator. Remove any fat that may congeal on top. Use as directed in recipe.

*This former French colony in Africa has markets that abound with spices which flavor this soup. A fine summer soup.*

## Cricket's

### VEAL CRICKET'S

12 (3-ounce) veal escalopines,
4 tablespoons clarified butter
¾ cup MUSHROOM DUXELLES
1½ cup MORNAY SAUCE
¾ cup DEMI-GLACE SAUCE
6 broccoli florets, garnish
6 cherry tomatoes, garnish
Watercress, garnish

1. Sauté veal lightly in clarified butter for 2 minutes on each side at medium-high heat. Place on dinner plates.
2. Spread Mushroom Duxelles over the veal. Top with Mornay Sauce.
3. Pour the Demi-glace Sauce around the edges.
4. Garnish with broccoli, cherry tomatoes and watercress.

### MUSHROOM DUXELLES

½ tablespoon chopped onion
1 tablespoon clarified butter
1 pound mushrooms
1 tablespoon Bechamel sauce

1. Sauté chopped onion in clarified butter at medium heat. Mix in chopped mushrooms. Sauté until the liquid has evaporated, stirring constantly.
2. Mix in Bechamel sauce, bringing to a boil. Remove from heat.

# CRICKET'S

### MORNAY SAUCE

| | |
|---|---|
| 3 tablespoons butter | Salt and pepper, to taste |
| 3 tablespoons flour | ½ cup Swiss cheese, grated |
| 1½ cups hot milk | 1 teaspoon Dijon mustard |
| 3 tablespoons heavy cream | |

1. Melt the butter in a saucepan at medium heat. Whisk in the flour. Continue to cook for about 4 to 5 minutes.
2. Whisk in the milk. Simmer for 3 to 4 minutes. Sauce should thicken. Mix in cream, salt and pepper to taste; add Swiss cheese and Dijon mustard.
3. Continue simmering until cheese has melted. Be careful the sauce does not brown. Use as directed.

*Before adding cream in step 2 save out 1 tablespoon and use as Bechamel Sauce in Mushroom Duxelles.*

### DEMI-GLACE SAUCE

| | |
|---|---|
| 5 to 6 pounds beef or veal bones, cracked | ½ teaspoon salt |
| 3 carrots, roughly chopped | ½ teaspoon freshly crushed peppercorns |
| 1 large onion, sliced | 3 tablespoons butter |
| ½ teaspoon thyme | 4 tablespoons flour |
| 2 to 3 bay leaves | ¼ cup Marsala |
| ¼ cup tomato puree | |

1. Preheat oven to 425°. Place bones, carrots, onion, thyme and bay leaves in a heavy roasting pan. Bake for 25 minutes or until brown.
2. Transfer ingredients to a large stock pot. Deglaze pan with a little water. Add tomato puree, salt and peppercorns. Cover with water. Simmer for 2½ hours. Skim as necessary. Strain with cheesecloth.
3. Melt butter in a heavy small skillet. Whisk in the flour. Cook for 5 minutes over medium heat. Stir occasionally. Slowly add mixture to strained stock. Simmer approximately 1 hour to reduce. Stir in Marsala.

# CRICKET'S

## HOT CABBAGE à la REIMS

- 1 head of cabbage, shredded
- 1 cup VINAIGRETTE DRESSING
- 2 tablespoons browned butter
- 2 tablespoons Demi-glace or Brown Sauce

1. Preheat oven to 500°.
2. Mix the shredded cabbage with Vinaigrette Dressing and the Demi-glace Sauce.
3. Place casserole in oven for 2 minutes.
4. Take casserole out of oven and drizzle butter over the cabbage.
5. To serve, drain excess liquid. Serve hot.

### VINAIGRETTE DRESSING

- 1 egg yolk
- 2 tablespoons Dijon Mustard
- 1 shallot, finely chopped
- 5 tablespoons red wine vinegar
- 10 tablespoons olive oil
- Salt, to taste
- Fresh ground pepper

Combine all the ingredients in a jar and shake to combine. Refrigerate until needed.

## CRICKET'S

### ROAST GOAT CHEESE

6 Crotins de Chavignolle goat cheese
1½ tablespoons olive oil
2 teaspoons fresh chopped herbs: basil, rosemary, thyme
6 slices sourdough bread, ¼" thick
Grape and grapevine leaves, garnish

1. Preheat oven to 500°.
2. Marinate Crotins in olive oil and chopped herbs for 4 to 6 hours at room temperature.
3. Toast bread on both sides.
4. Place Crotins in oven for 2 to 3 minutes. Spread over bread. Serve hot. Garnish with grapes and grapevine leaves.

### CHOCOLATE CAKE SANS FARINE

1 pound semi-sweet chocolate
3 tablespoons rum
3 tablespoons strong coffee
6 eggs
½ cup sugar
1 cup heavy cream
1 teaspoon vanilla
4 tablespoons sugar

1. Preheat oven to 350°.
2. Melt chocolate in the top of a double boiler over warm water.
3. Add rum and coffee to melted chocolate.
4. Beat eggs and sugar in a large bowl at high speed. Blend chocolate into the egg mixture, small amounts at a time.
5. Whip cream in a chilled bowl at high speed. Gradually add the sugar and vanilla. Continue beating until cream holds its shape. Fold cream into egg-chocolate mixture.
6. Spoon mixture into a greased and floured 9-inch springform pan. Bake for 1 hour. Reduce temperature to 100° and leave cake in for 30 minutes longer. Cool cake. Serve with whipped cream.

# L'ESCARGOT

*Dinner for Six*

*Ramequin of Crayfish*

*Fricassee de Lapin aux Racines*

*Mousse au Chocolat*

Wine:

With Crayfish, Pouilly Fume

With Fricassee, California Chardonnay

With Mousse, White Sauternes or Champagne

Lucien Verge, Owner/Chef

## L'Escargot

Award-winning French provencial cuisine has been the success for fifteen years at l'Escargot. From the moment that you enter the private side elevator that takes you to the dining room, to the moment you enter the warm interior, the excellence of your meal seems assured. The room is accented in a white and black color scheme with fine French posters hanging on the walls. The large partially draped windows expose the ever-changing excitement of Michigan Avenue.

Chef Verge trained in Lyon, France, moved to Paris and then to New York City in 1968. It was Chicago's gain when he decided to permanently reside here. L'Escargot, those wonderful small snails, he prepares with basil, garlic butter, linguini and cream. The fresh farm mussels he serves as a salad with French string beans, sliced red onions and an oil an vinegar dressing as well as in the shells with a garlic butter sauce.

701 North Michigan Avenue

# L'ESCARGOT

## RAMEQUIN OF CRAYFISH

- 50 live crayfish
- 2 ounces olive oil
- 3 ounces butter
- 1 garlic clove, crushed
- 3 shallots, chopped
- Bouquet Garni (1 bay leaf and 6 sprigs of parsley)
- 1 small carrot, julienned and blanched
- 1 small branch celery, julienned and blanched
- 1 cup dry sherry
- 1 cup fish stock or water
- Salt and white pepper
- 1 teaspoon tomato paste
- ½ pint whipping cream
- 1½ teaspoons cornstarch, dissolved in 2 tablespoons water
- Pinch saffron enfused in 1 tablespoon warm water
- 6 large mushroom caps, julienned

1. Wash crayfish in cold water. Devein each one as you would a shrimp. Rinse again. Sauté in hot olive oil in a large heavy skillet. Reserve.
2. Melt butter in separate skillet and slowly simmer garlic, shallots, Bouquet Garni, carrot, and celery. Remove Bouquet Garni.
3. Add crayfish and sherry and flame. Add water or stock, salt, pepper and tomato paste. Simmer 8 to 10 minutes. Remove crayfish and reserve.
4. Strain sauce, return to heat and reduce by half. Add cream and simmer 10 minutes. Thicken sauce with cornstarch/water mix, if desired. Add saffron. Check seasoning and consistency of sauce.
5. Sauté mushrooms in butter and add to sauce.
6. Unshell tail of crayfish. Mix crayfish into the sauce. Do not boil. Add julienne of carrot/celery.
7. Serve in small buttered ramequins.

*The slender dried stigmas of the crocus is the saffron that is used as a flavoring agent. Saffron has a light spicy and pungent taste. It is sometimes used as a coloring agent. It is the most expensive spice available. Crayfish, a freshwater shellfish, look like small lobsters.*

## L'ESCARGOT

### FRICASSEE de LAPIN aux RACINES

- 1 fresh rabbit, 3 to 4 pounds, cut into 12 pieces
- Salt and pepper
- 1 ounce olive oil
- 2 ounces butter
- 2 shallots, diced
- 1 medium-size onion, diced
- 1 large carrot, diced
- 1 clove garlic, crushed
- 10 ounces white wine
- 1 Bouquet Garni (2 leek leaves, 8 sprigs parsley, 1 bay leaf, 1 sprig thyme tied in cheesecloth)
- 1 (10½ ounce) can chicken consommé
- 1 pint whipping cream
- 2 teaspoons cornstarch, dissolved in 2 tablespoons water
- ¾ ounce apple brandy
- VEGETABLE GARNISH
- egg noodles

1. Season rabbit with salt and pepper.
2. Heat the oil in a heavy frying pan. Sauté rabbit pieces on both sides until golden brown. Drain, reserve.
3. Heat butter in frying pan. Sauté shallots, onion, carrot and garlic until soft but not browned. Pour vegetables over rabbit, stir. Add white wine and bouquet garni.
4. Simmer 3 minutes, add chicken consommé. Simmer 1½ hours or until tender. Remove meat, keep warm. Strain the sauce and return to the pan.
5. Add cream, bring mixture to a boil. Stir in diluted cornstarch and simmer 3 minutes. Check sauce to see if it is desired taste and thickness. Mix in apple brandy. Pour the sauce over the warm rabbit pieces.
6. Arrange Vegetable Garnish over the rabbit and serve with egg noodles.

*Rabbit can usually be obtained fully dressed from the butcher or supermarket. If cutting yourself, cut into twelve pieces: the two front legs, four pieces from the back legs, and two from the back. The rabbit has a light, delicate flavor; any over-seasoning will hide the original taste.*

## L'Escargot

### VEGETABLE GARNISH

- 2 leeks, white part only, julienned (use greens in Bouquet Garni)
- 2 shallots, minced
- 2 ounces butter
- 1 ounce white wine
- ¾ cup water
- 2 small carrots, julienned
- 1 medium-size celery root, julienned
- 4 small turnips, julienned
- 3 ounces butter

1. Sauté leeks and shallots in heated butter until soft. Add wine and continue cooking for 3 minutes, stirring continuously.
2. Add water, cover with piece of parchment paper and continue cooking until tender. Reserve.
3. Blanch carrots, celery root, and turnips. Heat butter in a large heavy skillet and sauté vegetables until soft. Combine carrots, celery and turnips with leeks and set aside.

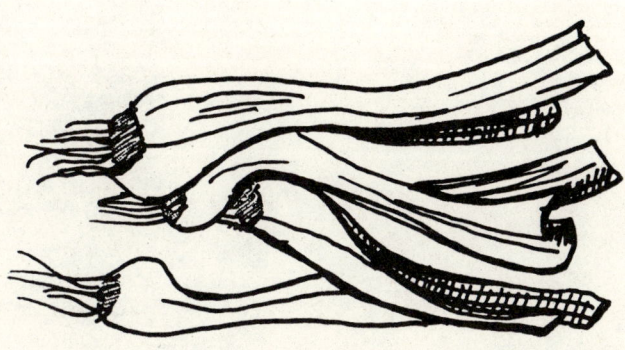

## L'Escargot

### MOUSSE au CHOCOLAT

| | |
|---|---|
| 4 ounces sweet chocolate | 1 stick soft butter |
| 4 ounces bitter chocolate |    (8 tablespoons) |
| ⅔ cup sugar | 2 tablespoons dark rum |
| ½ cup water | Pinch of salt |
| 5 eggs, separated | 1 cup whipping cream |

1. Melt chocolates in double boiler over warm water.
2. Boil sugar and water in heavy saucepan until sugar is dissolved and a syrup is formed, about 4 or 5 minutes.
3. Beat egg yolks until light. Gradually combine yolks into syrup, stirring constantly until thickened.
4. Add soft butter in pieces. Add melted chocolates and rum (or other liqueur of choice).
5. Beat egg whites with salt (or cream of tartar) at high speed until stiff. Stir a portion into chocolate mixture, then continue to fold in remaining egg whites.

## L'Escargot

6. Pour mousse in mold or glass bowl. Refrigerate 2 to 3 hours.
7. To serve, decorate with whipped cream, candied violets or oranges, or shaved chocolate.

*Eight ounces of semi-sweet chocolate may be substituted for the sweet and bitter. Whipped cream is never added to the mixture until it has chilled to a point where it is just starting to thicken. If it is added improperly it will not distribute evenly or may give a lumpy appearance.*

*Dinner for Six*

Roasted Peppers with Salami and Anchovies

Fettucine with Proscuitto, Peas and Cream

Sautéed Veal Chop Capriccio

White Chocolate Mousse

Wine:

With Peppers, Pinot di Pinot, Gancia

With Fettucine, 1980 Gavi dei Gavi, La Scolca Soldati

With Veal, 1979 Vermiglio, Costanti

With Dessert, Amaretto di Saronno

George Badonsky, Owner

Russell Bry, Chef

## GEORGE'S

George Badonsky, owner of the restaurant bearing his name, arrived at the restaurant business via a musical background. It is to this interest in music that we owe the outstanding jazz musicians that perform at the restaurant. The great love that George has for music, food and wine is shared with his guests.

The beautifully designed George's has won many awards including the coveted American Institute of Architects Award. Chicago Art and Architecture designed the smart, somewhat stark room with Italian green marble, curved glass block walls and undulating glass block bar.

Chef Russell Bry began his career with Badonsky in 1977. He has a classical training and worked with a catering group before coming to Chicago.

It is here at George's that one can appreciate the fine cuisine of northern Italy: fresh fish, the light sauces, pasta cooked just right and served with many epicurean combinations or veal chops served with marinated tomatos. An excellent selection of Italian wines makes all complete.

230 West Kinzie

## GEORGE'S

### ROASTED PEPPERS with SALAMI and ANCHOVIES

    6  large, firm sweet red peppers
    1  large clove garlic, crushed
  ¼  cup lemon juice
  ½  cup virgin olive oil
       Salt and white pepper
  12  pieces salami, thinly sliced
  12  anchovy fillets

1. Core and seed peppers. Place directly over gas flame or under broiler of your stove until all sides are charred.
2. Peel peppers under running cold water and discard skin.
3. Place peppers in a bowl containing garlic, lemon juice, olive oil, salt and pepper. Allow to marinate for a minimum of 4 hours in refrigerator.
4. Arrange 2 slices of salami on side of each plate. Place one pepper in the center of each plate. Criss-cross the 2 anchovy fillets atop pepper.

*It was the cuisine of northern Italy that led the world in gastronomic arts. It was this art that Catherine brought along with her to the court of France. It was this treasure of cooking that led to the development of French cuisine as we know it today.*

## GEORGE'S

### FETTUCINE with PROSCIUTTO, PEAS, and CREAM

- 2 cups heavy whipping cream
- 3 tablespoons butter
- 1¼ cup grated Romano or Asiago cheese
- ¾ cup julienne-cut Prosciutto
- ¾ cup fresh peas, cooked
- 2 pounds egg fettucine
- Ground black pepper

1. Place cream and butter in a large sauté pan and bring to a boil.
2. Add 1 cup grated cheese and whip with a whisk until mixture is smooth and has thickened.
3. Add prosciutto and peas; return to a boil.
4. Add cooked fettucine and toss until well heated.
5. Serve on warm plates. Garnish with grated cheese and fresh ground pepper.

### SAUTÉED VEAL CHOPS CAPRICCIO

- 6 (8–10 ounce) veal chops
- Flour
- 3 eggs, slightly beaten
- 2 cups milk
- Salt and pepper, to taste
- 4 cups bread crumbs
- 4 tablespoons salad oil
- 4 tablespoons olive oil
- TOMATO GARNISH

1. Preheat oven to 400°.
2. Pound veal chops thin, to about ⅛-inch thickness. Lightly dust with flour.
3. Combine eggs, milk, salt and pepper to taste in a bowl. Dip veal chops in egg wash and into bread crumbs.
4. Heat oils in large heavy skillet. Sauté veal chops until golden brown on both sides. Do not overcook.
5. Place veal chops on a sheet pan and bake for 8 minutes. Place chops on warmed plates and top with chilled Tomato Garnish.

# George's

## TOMATO GARNISH

- 3 large firm ripe tomatoes, diced
- ¼ cup diced onion
- 2 cloves garlic, minced
- ¼ cup olive oil
- ¼ cup red wine vinegar

1. Mix all ingredients well in a bowl. Cover.
2. Refrigerate until needed.

## WHITE CHOCOLATE MOUSSE

- 4 egg yolks
- 1 tablespoon vanilla
- ¼ cup sugar
- ¼ cup white wine
- 12 ounces white chocolate, melted
- 1 quart heavy whipping cream
- 1 ounce dark chocolate, shaved

1. Mix egg yolks, vanilla, sugar and white wine in top of double boiler over warm water. Whisk until mixture forms a thin ribbon in the bowl. Remove from heat.
2. Add melted chocolate and mix well. Cool.
3. Whip cream until stiff. Fold into cooled chocolate mixture.
4. Pour mousse into chilled glasses and refrigerate until set.
5. Garnish with dark chocolate shavings.

*White chocolate is really not chocolate because it contains no chocolate liquor. It is high in cocoa butter and is used for mousses, frostings, fillings, cakes and dipping. Always buy the best quality chocolate.*

# Gordon

*Dinner for Six*

*Eggplant Duxelle with Roquefort Glaze*

*Mussel Chowder*

*Steamed Lake Trout with Tomato Soy Sauce*

*Cucumber and Onion Salad with Raspberry Vinaigrette*

*Drunken Fruit Compote*

*Wine:*

*A Dry California Chenin Blanc*

*Gordon Sinclair, Owner*

*John Terczak, Chef*

## Gordon

This ninety-seat pocket of New York City ambiance opened in 1976 in one of Chicago's less than glossy neighborhoods, Clark Street north of the Loop, an area that currently is undergoing a renaissance in popularity. A small, intimate restaurant, Gordon highlights fresh seafoods served with fine light natural sauces. The menu is balanced by options of lamb, veal, pork and poultry dishes which change with the four seasons. A handsome thirty-seat lounge features entertainment on weekends.

The cuisine is quite simple and prepared with a light touch. It is varied and yet delicate, and tastes as good as it looks. Main courses are served with an interesting salad and fresh vegetables that are first steamed on the crispy side, then sautéed. All desserts are prepared on the premises and all foods are purchased fresh daily. Some herbs are grown in the restaurant and snipped at the time they are needed. An excellent selection of more than six dozen wines is available. The menu changes daily, even from lunch to dinner.

Owner Gordon Sinclair is a native of Flint, Michigan. He moved to New York City in 1970 to work for a consulting firm and later an advertising agency. In 1973 he returned to Chicago to head the public relations department of a daily newspaper. One year later he took a part-time job at a local restaurant as captain and maitre d' to test his liking for the business. The rest is history.

512 North Clark

## GORDON

### EGGPLANT DUXELLE with ROQUEFORT GLAZE

- 1 pound mushrooms, sliced
- 3 tablespoons clarified butter
- 2 large Bermuda onions, diced
- 3 tablespoons tomato paste
- Salt and pepper
- 2 medium-size eggplants
- 2 cups olive oil
- 2 cups HOLLANDAISE SAUCE
- 1 cup BECHAMEL SAUCE
- 3–4 ounces Roquefort cheese, crumbled

1. Preheat oven to 350°.
2. Sauté mushrooms in half of butter until soft in a heavy skillet; drain; dry. Finely chop mushrooms and wring them out in a towel.
3. Sauté onions in remaining butter until soft in a heavy skillet. Combine onions, mushrooms and tomato paste. Season with salt and pepper.
4. Cut eggplants across in ¾-inch pieces. Season with salt and pepper. Sauté eggplant in hot olive oil until eggplant is cooked half way. Remove eggplant and pat dry.
5. Distribute the mushroom/onion duxelle evenly over the six slices of eggplant. Place eggplants on a cookie sheet and bake for about 5 to 8 minutes.
6. Remove from the oven and transfer to a gratin serving dish.
7. Combine the two sauces and pour them over the eggplants. Sprinkle with Roquefort.
8. Place the serving dish under the broiler and broil until they are brown and bubbly. Remove, sprinkle with chopped parsley and serve.

*Eggplant has been cultivated in France since the beginning of the 17th century. Eggplant originated in India and is known in France as Aubergine.*

## Gordon's

### HOLLANDAISE SAUCE

½ cup butter, creamed, room temperature
4 egg yolks
1 tablespoon freshly squeezed lemon juice
Salt
2 tablespoons boiling water

1. Place creamed butter in the top of a double boiler, over warm water. Beat in the egg yolks.
2. Mix in the lemon juice and salt. Whisk in the boiling water. Stir constantly until the sauce thickens.

### BECHAMEL SAUCE

3 tablespoons butter
1 small onion, minced
3 tablespoons flour
2½ to 3 cups hot milk
Salt and pepper

1. Heat butter in 1-quart saucepan and sauté onions until lightly brown over medium heat. Whisk in flour.
2. Mix in milk, salt and pepper, whisking constantly, until mixture is desired consistency.

## MUSSEL CHOWDER

25 to 30 New England mussels, well scrubbed
1 quart chicken stock or WHITE VEAL STOCK
4 cups dry white wine
1 teaspoon dried thyme
¼ cup clarified butter
1 cup diced onion
1 cup diced carrot
1 cup diced celery
1 tablespoon minced garlic
1 cup chopped tomato
1 pint heavy cream
Salt, pepper, Tabasco

1. In a stock pot, steam the mussels in a combination of chicken or Veal Stock, wine and thyme. When they open, remove. Reserve the steaming liquid. Remove mussel meat from the shells. Discard the shells. Set meat aside. Discard any unopened mussels.
2. Sauté onions, carrots, celery, garlic in clarified butter in a large saucepan until vegetables are soft. Mix in the mussel meat, stock and tomato. Bring to a boil and reduce by one-third.
3. Reduce the cream by half in a separate saucepan. Add to the soup. Season with salt, pepper and Tabasco. Serve hot.

*Mussels are an edible mollusk found in all the oceans of the world, especially in cold regions, as off the coast of Maine.*

## VEAL STOCK

3½ pounds veal bones
1 small onion, sliced
1 clove garlic, crushed
1 small carrot, sliced
1 stalk celery, sliced
½ teaspoon salt, pepper

1. Place bones, vegetables, salt and pepper in one gallon of water and bring to a boil. Reduce heat and continue to simmer for 45 minutes to an hour. Strain stock.
2. Skim off any scum that may rise to the surface. Return stock to pot and continue cooking for 1 hour or until stock is reduced to about 1 quart.

## GORDON

### STEAMED LAKE TROUT with TOMATO SOY SAUCE

    6 (6–8 ounce) lake trout fillets
    TOMATO SOY SAUCE
    Pickled ginger
    Sesame seeds

    1 cucumber, peeled and thinly sliced
    Oba leaves, available at Oriental food stores

1. Place trout fillets on a perforated pan over simmering water with a sealable lid and steam until watery mucus exudes from the trout. This indicates fish is done, but still juicy. Remove from pan and place on serving dish.
2. Ladle sauce on top.
3. Garnish with pieces of pickled ginger, sesame seeds and cucumber. Sprinkle fish with freshly chopped oba leaves.

## Gordon

### TOMATO SOY SAUCE

- 4 tablespoons butter
- ¾ pound mushrooms, sliced
- 1 large onion, diced
- ¼ cup chicken stock
- ⅓ cup soy sauce
- 2 tablespoons cornstarch mixed with ½ cup cold water
- 3 tomatoes, peeled, seeded, chopped (about 2 cups)
- Pepper, to taste
- Fresh lemon juice, to taste

1. Sauté mushrooms in half of butter and onions in half separately. Drain each.
2. Place stock, mushrooms, onions and soy sauce in a saucepan and bring to a boil. Add cornstarch mixture and return to a boil. Reduce by one-third. Remove any scum that forms.
3. Remove from heat and add tomatoes. Season with pepper and lemon juice.

## GORDON

### CUCUMBER and ONION SALAD with RASPBERRY VINAIGRETTE

4 cucumbers, peeled, sliced
2 purple onions, sliced paper thin
1 bunch fresh mint, chopped
RASPBERRY VINAIGRETTE

1. Arrange the cucumbers in a circular overlapping pattern on individual serving plates with the onions strewn on top.
2. Drizzle dressing on top of vegetables. Sprinkle with mint.

#### RASPBERRY VINAIGRETTE

½ cup raspberry vinegar
1 cup salad oil
5 shallots, chopped

Combine ingredients in a jar, cover and shake to combine. Refrigerate until ready to use.

## GORDON

### DRUNKEN FRUIT COMPOTE

- 1 cup sugar
- ½ cup water
- 3 cups Rainwater Madeira
- 1½ cups white creme de menthe
- ¾ cup maraschino cherry brandy
- 1 cup fresh-squeezed orange juice
- ½ cup fresh-squeezed lemon juice
- 1 pint strawberries, hulled
- ½ pint blueberries
- 4 cups sliced ripe peaches
- 1½ cups sour cream
- ¾ teaspoon nutmeg
- 6 sprigs fresh wintergreen

1. Boil the sugar and water until fully dissolved, about 5 minutes.
2. Place mixture in a large glass bowl. Add the three liqueurs and the two citrus juices and mix.
3. Wash all fruit and marinate in liqueur/juice mixture overnight.
4. Divide the fruits and juices among large, footed glasses. Garnish with sour cream and nutmeg. Finish with a sprig of wintergreen.

歡迎

# House of Hunan

*Dinner for Six*

*Hot and Sour Soup*

*Noodle Salad*

*Five Spice Beef*

*Spicy Szechwan Snails*

*Yu Hsiang Chee Pien*
*(Chicken with Garlic Sauce)*

*Willow Beef*

*Lake Tungting Smelt*

*Wine:*

*Wan Fu*

*George Kuan, Owner*

## House of Hunan

The House of Hunan is an epicurean tour of China—all under one roof. Here one can travel from the hot, spicy western regions of Hunan and Szechwan to the sweet, rich eastern region surrounding Shanghai; from the milder, but richly varied southern region around Canton to the eclectic, exquisite cuisine that has evolved around the northern capital of Beijing.

The hot red chilis and peppercorns have given the cuisine of Hunan and Szechwan the reputation of being paralyzing to the palate. In fact, only every-day dishes in Szechwan are highly flavored. Formal dinners are very mild as no peppers are served at all. The central characteristic of this western cuisine is intricacy; most dishes contain an elaborate weaving of sweet, sour, bitter, hot, salty, aromatic and fragrant flavors. Extra-spicy dishes are marked HOT! on the menu for those devotees. Diners with more delicate palates may request "No peppers."

The cuisine of the eastern port of Shanghai is rich in fish and seafood and more gently spiced than to the west—primarily with sugar and soy sauce. Vegetables abound in these dishes.

The southern school from around Canton is most familiar to Americans. Seafood, unusual delicacies and vegetables characterize the food, while stir-frying and blanching is the most noted technique.

The Mandarin style stems from the northern area around the capital Beijing. For over a millenium Imperial chefs have honed the essence of culinary China for the residents of the Forbidden City. Thus this is the richest style of all.

The House of Hunan provides the diner with an opportunity to explore the world's most varied and complex cuisine.

535 North Michigan Avenue

## HOUSE OF HUNAN

### HOT AND SOUR SOUP

- 2 to 4 dried black mushrooms
- 6 to 8 dried tree ear mushrooms
- 1 tablespoon peanut oil
- 4 ounces pork, shredded (lean butt is recommended)
- 4 ounces bamboo shoots, diced finely
- 5 to 6 cups chicken broth
- 1 tablespoon soy sauce
- Salt
- 2 tablespoons cornstarch
- ½ cup fresh tofu, diced in ½" cubes
- 2 eggs, slightly beaten
- 2 tablespoons white vinegar
- 1 tablespoon sesame oil
- 1 tablespoon white pepper
- 1 green onion, minced

1. Soak black and tree ear mushrooms in hot water for 30 minutes or until softened. Cut off the tough stems and shred.
2. Heat the oil in a wok until almost smoking. Add shredded pork. Stir to separate and cook until brown, about 1 minute or so.
3. Mix in bamboo shoots and mushrooms. Stir to combine. Add broth and soy sauce; continue stirring. Sprinkle with salt to taste. Bring to a boil, reduce to simmer.
4. Dissolve cornstarch in 3 tablespoons cold water. Stir mixture into soup. When soup has thickened, add tofu cubes and bring to a boil again. Reduce to simmer and stir in slightly beaten eggs in a slow steady stream so as to make eggs thread. Soup can be made in advance to this point.
5. When ready to serve, reheat soup. Add white vinegar, sesame oil, white pepper and green onions. Stir and serve.

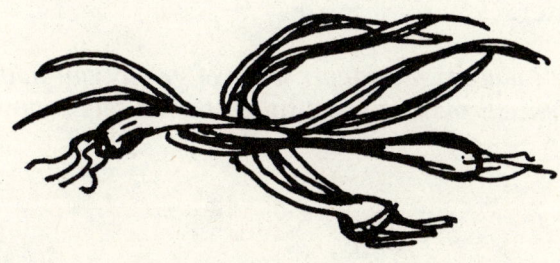

## HOUSE OF HUNAN

### NOODLE SALAD

- 1 large chicken breast
- 2 sheets Tientsin Fen P'i wrappers, available at Oriental food stores
- 2 teaspoons salt
- 1 cucumber
- 2 tablespoons shredded baked ham
- ¼ cup rice wine or dry sherry
- 2 tablespoons light soy sauce
- 1½ tablespoons vinegar
- 2 teaspoons sesame oil
- 1 tablespoon dry mustard
- 2 tablespoons sesame paste, diluted with 2 tablespoons of chicken broth

1. Add chicken to 2 quarts of boiling water in a 5- to 6-quart saucepan. Simmer for 5 minutes. Remove from heat. Allow chicken to stand in stock for additional 15 minutes. Remove chicken from stock and allow to cool. When chicken is cool, bone and shred into toothpick-size strips. Reserve.
2. Soak wrappers in hot water for 30 minutes to reconstitute. Cut into half-inch-wide strips. Rub with 1 teaspoon of salt. Reserve.
3. Peel cucumber, remove seeds. Cut into toothpick-size strips. Rub with 1 teaspoon salt and set aside for 30 minutes.
4. Wash salt off wrappers and cucumber; drain.
5. Combine chicken and ham in a large mixing bowl.
6. Combine wine, soy sauce, vinegar and sesame oil in a small bowl. Add mustard and sesame paste and blend.
7. Add cucumbers and wrappers to chicken and ham. Toss with mustard/sesame paste dressing so as to thoroughly coat. Remove to a serving platter.

*Tientsin Fen P'i is a dried wrapper made of green bean flour. Cellophane noodles or vermicelli may be substituted. Six or seven ounces of noodles works well.*

## HOUSE OF HUNAN

### FIVE SPICE BEEF

- 2 whole star anise
- 1 2"-piece of dried tangerine peel
- 1 teaspoon fennel seeds
- 1 4"-piece Chinese cinnamon bark
- 1 tablespoon whole Szechwan peppercorns
- 1 ½"-piece ginger, peeled, crushed
- 1 cup dark soy sauce
- ½ cup light soy sauce
- ¼ cup sugar
- ¼ cup rice wine
- 5 cups water
- 2 pounds boneless beef shank
- 1 teaspoon sesame oil

1. Prepare a spice bundle by wrapping star anise, dried tangerine peel, fennel seeds, cinnamon bark, peppercorns and ginger in a double layer of cheesecloth.
2. Combine soy sauces, sugar, wine, water and spice bundle in a 4- to 5-quart saucepan. Stir mixture and bring to a boil. Reduce to simmer and continue cooking for 30 minutes.
3. Rinse beef shank, blanch with boiling water. Place in marinade, simmer for 2 hours. Remove beef from pan and cool 30 minutes. Refrigerate.
4. When ready to serve, brush beef with sesame oil to glaze. Slice thinly and serve.

*The marinade may be used to prepare all sorts of "Five Spice" dishes, including chicken, duck, squab, eggs, pork, mushrooms, bean curd, chicken gizzards and liver. Five Spice Eggs is a popular picnic dish. They are made by simmering hard-boiled eggs, that have been shelled, in a pot of the marinade for 30 minutes. Allow to cool for 15 minutes before chilling.*

## HOUSE OF HUNAN

### SPICY SZECHWAN SNAILS

- 3 tablespoons vegetable oil
- 3 tablespoons minced garlic
- 3 tablespoons grated ginger
- 1 pound (7 dozen) escargot
- SEASONING SAUCE
- ½ cup rice wine or dry sherry
- 2 cups chicken broth
- 2 green onions, minced
- 2 tablespoons cornstarch, dissolved in 2 tablespoons cold water
- 1 tablespoon sesame oil

1. Heat the oil to almost smoking in a wok over high heat. Add garlic and ginger and stir-fry about 30 seconds. Add snails and stir to combine. Add Seasoning Sauce, rice wine, chicken broth and green onions. Stir ingredients so as to coat snails, about 2 minutes.
2. Add cornstarch mixture. When sauce has thickened, stir in sesame oil. Remove snails to a serving plate. Cover each with a spoonful of sauce and serve.

### *SEASONING SAUCE*

- 2 tablespoons Szechwan chili sauce
- 3 tablespoons Chinese barbecue sauce (Satay)
- 1 tablespoon black beans, rinsed
- ½ teaspoon salt
- 1 tablespoon sugar
- 1 teaspoon white pepper
- 2 tablespoons soy sauce

Combine all ingredients. Reserve.

# HOUSE OF HUNAN

## YU HSIANG CHEE PIEN

- 2 to 3 dried black wood ear mushrooms
- 1 whole chicken breast, skinned, boned, thinly sliced
- 1 tablespoon cornstarch
- 1 tablespoon soy sauce
- 2 cups vegetable oil
- 1 garlic clove, minced
- 2 teaspoons minced ginger
- 6 water chestnuts, sliced
- 1 small red pepper, sliced
- 1 small green pepper, sliced
- 1 small bamboo shoot, sliced
- SEASONING SAUCE
- 1 green onion shredded
- 1 teaspoon sesame oil
- ¼ teaspoon black pepper

1. Soak mushrooms in hot water for 30 minutes to soften. Cut off tough stems.
2. Slice chicken in short ½-inch-wide strips. Place in mixing bowl, add 1 tablespoon cornstarch and 1 tablespoon soy sauce. Set aside for 30 minutes.
3. Heat oil in a wok to almost smoking or about 375°. Add chicken and deep fry until chicken turns white. Carefully remove with a slotted spoon. Drain. Cool oil.
4. Remove all but 3 tablespoons of the oil; reheat. Stir in garlic and ginger. Stir-fry 30 seconds. Add mushrooms, water chestnuts, peppers and bamboo shoots. Stir-fry until vegetables are crisp-tender, about 1½ minutes. Add the cooked chicken. Mix in Seasoning Sauce. Stir until all ingredients are coated with the Sauce.
5. Stir in green onions. Add sesame oil. Season with pepper. Serve.

### SEASONING SAUCE

- 1 tablespoon soy sauce
- 1 tablespoon Chinese brown vinegar (cider vinegar may be substituted)
- 1 tablespoon hot pepper paste
- ½ tablespoon rice wine or dry sherry
- 1 teaspoon sugar
- 1 teaspoon cornstarch

Combine all ingredients. Reserve until needed.

## HOUSE OF HUNAN

Dried Oriental ingredients, such as black wood ear mushrooms, are stored in jars or plastic bags and kept in a cool dry area. The wood ear mushrooms are small, crinkled, dried tree fungus. They must be soaked in hot water to reconstitute before use. They will expand two to three times their original size. The mushrooms are soft and resilient in texture and have a subtle taste.

### WILLOW BEEF

- 8 ounces filet mignon, thinly sliced in 1" lengths
- ½ teaspoon Chinese barbecue sauce (Satay)
- 1 teaspoon light soy sauce
- 1 teaspoon rice wine or dry sherry
- 2 egg whites, slightly beaten
- ¼ teaspoon Five Spice powder
- 2 tablespoons vegetable oil
- 1 whole dried red pepper, seeded
- ¼ teaspoon minced garlic
- ½ teaspoon minced ginger
- ½ teaspoon minced green onions

SEASONING SAUCE
- 1 tablespoon cornstarch, dissolved in 2 tablespoons cold water
- 1 bunch watercress, trimmed

1. Combine marinade ingredients: barbecue sauce, soy sauce, rice wine, egg whites and Five Spice powder. Add beef and marinate for 2 hours at room temperature. Remove beef and drain.
2. Heat 1 tablespoon of oil in wok. Add beef and stir to separate. Fry until meat has cooked, about 3 minutes. Remove and drain.
3. Add other tablespoon of oil to wok and heat. Add red peppers and fry about 30 seconds. Add garlic, ginger and green onions. Stir-fry about 1 minute.
4. Add Seasoning Sauce. Return beef to wok. Mix well.
5. Add cornstarch mixture. Stir-fry to thicken.
6. Blanch fresh watercress by dipping in boiling water; drain. Arrange on serving platter and place beef over watercress.

# HOUSE OF HUNAN

## SEASONING SAUCE

- ½ cup chicken stock
- 1 tablespoon rice wine or dry sherry
- 1 teaspoon sugar
- 1 teaspoon oyster sauce
- 2 teaspoons soy sauce
- 1 tablespoon cornstarch, dissolved in 2 tablespoons cold water

Combine all ingredients. Reserve until needed.

Because of the speed at which Chinese food cooks and the variability of individual stoves, there may be slight variances in the cooking time.

## HOUSE OF HUNAN

### LAKE TUNGTING SMELT

- 1 pound smelts
- 3 to 4 tablespoons soy sauce
- 3 tablespoons Chinese rice wine or dry sherry
- 1 1"-piece of ginger, minced
- 1 to 2 garlic cloves, minced
- 2 to 3 green onions, minced
- Salt
- 1 cup cornstarch
- 1 teaspoon ground black pepper
- 2 to 3 cups vegetable oil
- 1 tablespoon Chinese brown vinegar (cider vinegar can be used)
- 2 to 3 tablespoons tomato puree
- 1 to 2 teaspoons sugar
- 1 tablespoon dried tangerine peel, flaked into tiny pieces
- 1 whole dried red pepper, chopped into small pieces, seeded
- 1 tablespoon sesame oil

1. Clean smelt and pat dry. Marinate for 30 minutes in soy, wine, ginger, garlic, green onion and salt. Remove fish and drain. Reserve marinade.
2. Dust smelt with cornstarch and black pepper. Coat completely and shake off excess.

3. Heat oil in a wok until almost smoking. Add fish and deep fry until golden brown. Remove with slotted spoon. Allow to drain thoroughly on paper toweling. Fry in batches so as not to lower temperature of oil. When done, remove all oil except 2 to 3 tablespoons.
4. Add marinade to wok. Mix in vinegar, tomato puree, sugar, tangerine peel and pepper. Stir thoroughly and bring to a boil. Reduce heat and allow to simmer until thick. Add sesame oil.
5. Return fish to wok, toss lightly to coat and serve.

*If smelt are fried perfectly, the bones are crispy and edible. Around the shores of Lake Michigan the smelt are best in the spring.*

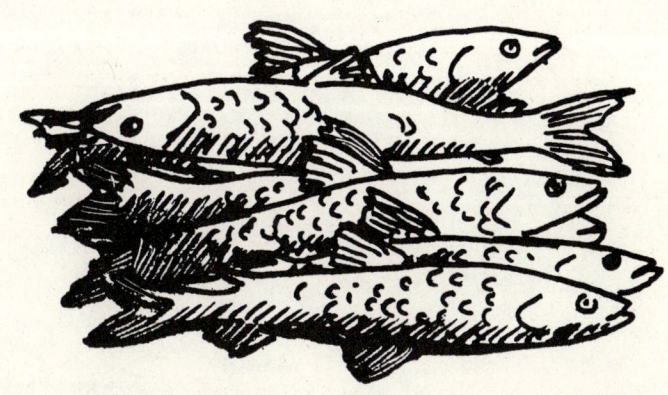

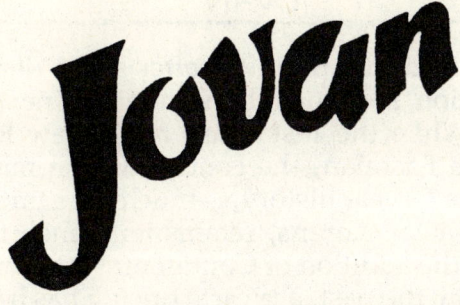

*Dinner for Six*

*Snail, Sweetbread and Goat Cheese Ravioli*

*Brie Soup "Jean La Font"*

*Rolled Pheasant with Pinenuts and Cabbage*

*Jovan Dinner Salad*

*Grand Marnier Souffle*

*Wine:*

*With Appetizer, 1982 Sancerre*

*With Pheasant, Vosne Romanee, 1978*

*Dieter Ahrens, Owner*

*Jeff Jackson, Chef*

## JOVAN

Jovan, which closed in April 1982 after a fire destroyed its Near North Side location, reopened this spring in its new location just off Lincoln Park. While the restaurant has a new look, created by designer Jerome Eastman, the concept which made it a popular place to dine over its 14-year history, is much the same. The menu, according to owner Dieter Ahrens, retains its French flavor but it has been updated with the addition of Continental and American dishes.

In a departure from the past, à la carte pricing has been added to the menu, offering an alternative to Jovan's traditional price fixe menu. Ahrens made this change, he said, "Because we felt some people who dine early or are watching calories aren't interested in five-course dinners. This way people can order just what they wish and their companions can have a choice of either a five-course dinner or ordering à la carte."

Eastman has designed an intimate and comfortable setting for Jovan's new location. Now there are four distinct dining areas. At the center is a bar that seats some two dozen. The dining areas radiate from this hub. Sconces mounted on the columns that run along all three windowed walls provide soft illumination. Jovan is alive and well.

1660 North LaSalle Drive

## JOVAN

### SNAIL, SWEETBREAD AND GOAT CHEESE RAVIOLI

Filling:
- ½ pound butter
- 3 ounces minced shallots
- 2 ounces minced garlic
- Salt and pepper
- 1 ounce chopped parsley
- 18 snails
- ¾ pound sweetbreads, sliced
- 4 ounces olive oil
- 3½ ounces goat cheese

Dough:
- 2½ cups flour
- Salt and pepper
- 3 eggs
- 1 ounce olive oil

1. For Filling: Melt butter and cook shallots and garlic until tender. Add salt, pepper and parsley.
2. In a sauté pan, sauté snails and sweetbreads separately in the olive oil. Drain in a colander. Add both to shallot mixture and allow to cool. When cool, add the crumbled goat cheese.
3. For Dough: Combine flour, salt and pepper in a large bowl.
4. Mix eggs and olive oil together and incorporate into flour. Knead into a smooth dough. Cover with a cloth and let rest 1 hour.
5. To Assemble: Roll dough very thin and lay out on a sheet pan.
6. Place three snails in 2 ounces of sweetbread/goat cheese mixture in piles spaced evenly apart in rows on the dough.
7. Brush an egg wash around the piles and lay a second thinly rolled piece of dough over the top.
8. Press firmly around each ravioli. Cut into squares so that each pile is enclosed in the sealed dough.
9. Poach raviolis in salted and oiled water until tender. Pat dry and serve immediately with your favorite tomato sauce.

*Sweetbread is a ductless gland situated in the upper part of the thorax. The sweetbread of the calf and lamb are usually selected for this delicacy.*

## JOVAN

### BRIE SOUP "JEAN LA FONT"

| | |
|---|---|
| 1 leek, white part only, sliced | ¾ quart chicken stock |
| 4 ounces butter | 1 pint cream |
| ½ pound mushrooms, sliced | 1 tablespoons cornstarch |
| 4 scallions, minced | ½ pound Brie |
| 6 ounces pale dry or Amontillado sherry | 6 croutons |

1. Sweat leek in butter until tender. Add mushrooms and scallions.
2. Mix in 4 ounces sherry and reduce by half. Add chicken stock and bring to a boil. Add cream and return to a boil.
3. Dilute cornstarch in 2 ounces of sherry and add to the soup. Simmer 20 minutes. Season with salt and pepper.
4. Slice Brie thin and place one slice on each crouton. Place one crouton atop each of 6 bowls filled with the soup.
5. Place bowls under the broiler; melt cheese. Serve immediately.

### ROLLED PHEASANT with PINENUTS and CABBAGE

| | |
|---|---|
| 3 pheasants, 2½ to 3 pounds each | Salt and pepper |
| ½ pound lardons | PHEASANT JUICE |
| 2 small heads cabbage, cut into 2" pieces, blanched | Pinenuts, roasted |

1. Preheat oven to 425°.
2. Bone out the pheasant, starting at breast bone and working down to the leg. Leave all the skin on. Remove the leg and reserve for cabbage. Bone out the meat from thigh and place in center of breast. Roll skin around and tie, forming a ballottine.

## JOVAN

3. Brown pheasant legs and lardons in a pot. Add the blanched cabbage. Cover and braise slowly. Season to taste with salt and pepper.
4. Season the rolled pheasant and brown on one side. Turn over and roast in oven until medium.
5. Remove when cooked and let rest 5 minutes.
6. Arrange cabbage on plate. Slice pheasant and lay it out on the cabbage. Cover with Pheasant Juice and sprinkle with toasted pinenuts.

### PHEASANT JUICE

| | | |
|---|---|---|
| | pheasant bones | Pinch thyme |
| 1 | onion | 1 bay leaf |
| ½ | carrot | 6 black peppercorns |
| 1 | celery rib | Chicken stock |

1. Brown pheasant bones and place in a large stock pot with vegetables and herbs. Cover with chicken stock and simmer 3 hours.
2. Skim fat when necessary. Strain stock; keep warm until used.

*According to Larousse Gastronomique, the ballottine is made of a piece of meat, fowl, game or fish which is boned, stuffed and rolled into the shape of a bundle. A ballottine decribes a kind of galantine served as a hot entree.*

*Lardon in this sense is salt pork which is skinned and cut in strips ¼" × ¼" × 1" long. The lardons are poached in water until tender. The poaching also removes the saltiness from the salt pork.*

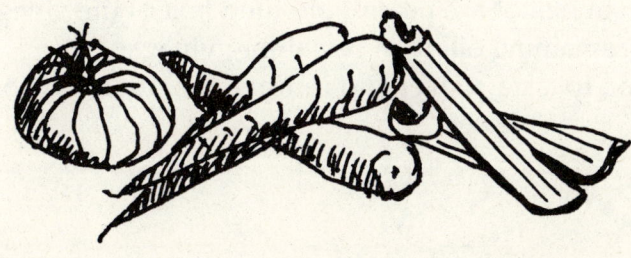

## JOVAN

### JOVAN DINNER SALAD

1 jicama
1 small head curly endive
1 small head Boston lettuce
1 carrot, julienned
2 ribs celery, julienned
1 small zucchini, julienned
1 small yellow squash, julienned
JOVAN DRESSING
2 tomatoes, peeled, seeded, diced

1. Peel the jicama and slice thin. Place a slice on each plate.
2. Tear lettuces in small pieces and place in a large bowl along with the julienned vegetables. Toss with dressing.
3. Place tossed vegetables on top of jicama slice and decorate with tomatoes.

*Jicama is a woody-root vegetable, served regularly south of the border. It is usually eaten raw in salads and resembles a potato in texture.*

### JOVAN DRESSING

1 tablespoon grainy mustard
1 egg
1 tablespoon minced shallots
2 cloves garlic, minced
1 cup peanut oil
1 tablespoon sherry wine vinegar
Salt and pepper, to taste

1. Put mustard and egg in mixing bowl with shallots and garlic.
2. Whip in half of the peanut oil, then half of the vinegar.
3. Add remaining oil, then remaining vinegar.
4. Season to taste. Cover and refrigerate until ready to use.

## JOVAN

### GRAND MARNIER SOUFFLÉ

| | |
|---|---|
| 2 egg yolks | 1 cup scalded milk |
| 1 whole egg | 1 ounce butter |
| ¼ cup sugar | 3 ounces Grand Marnier |
| 1 teaspoon vanilla | ¼ cup toasted almonds |
| 4 tablespoons cornstarch | 12 egg whites |
| 4 tablespoons flour | ½ cup powdered sugar |

1. Preheat oven to 425°.
2. Combine yolks, egg, sugar, vanilla in the top of a double boiler. Whip until warm and sugar is dissolved. Add cornstarch and flour. Whip until thickened slightly, about 3 to 5 minutes.
3. Transfer mixture to a mixing bowl. Add butter and milk. Beat with electric beater until thick. Cool.
4. Combine egg base, Grand Marnier and toasted almonds in a bowl. In another bowl, whip egg whites and sugar until soft peaks form. Fold gently into the Grand Marnier base.
5. Pour mixture into a 1-quart souffle dish which has been buttered and sugared.
6. Bake in a water bath for 35 minutes. Dust with powdered sugar before serving warm.

## LEXANDER

*Dinner for Six*

Veal Tartar and Pasta Salad

Cream of Chili Soup

Roast Fillet of Peppered Pork with Brandy Sauce

Chinese Cabbage Salad with Buttermilk Dressing

Banana Split Meringue

*Wine:*

Gewürztraminer

Gordon Sinclair, Owner

John Terczak, Chef

## Lexander

Open since March 1981, Lexander has quickly gained a loyal following and a reputation for its innovative and imaginative menu featuring nouvelle American dishes served in a stylishly informal setting. The decor of the sixty-seat, two-story restaurant is as unusual as its menu. The walls and ceiling are virtually giant easels which display a combination of trompe l'oeil, surrealistic and faux marble techniques, creating the effect of dining outdoors in a fantasy world. Among the daily offerings are unusual pastas, whole fish, seafoods, beef tenderloin with raspberry red wine sauce, medallions of lamb with vegetables in a basil-garlic sauce and sautéed chicken breast with sweet mustard sauce. The food is strictly down-to-earth though, with menus featuring Chef John Terczak's country-style versions of classic dishes.

The care of the kitchen is under the watchful eye of the master de cuisine and part-owner John Terczak, a native of Detroit. He came to Chicago in 1958 and began studying cooking. In 1976 he became the chef de cuisine at Gordon Restaurant shortly after it opened. The menus he designs change daily and feature mostly fresh fish and seafood. Quality is not compromised.

508 North Clark Street

## LEXANDER

### VEAL TARTAR and PASTA SALAD

| | |
|---|---|
| 1 pound veal, finely ground | Salt and pepper |
| 1½ lemons, juice only | 12 full leaves Boston lettuce, washed and dried |
| 1 tablespoon spicy Dijon mustard | PASTA SALAD |
| | PASTA SALAD DRESSING |
| 1 small Bermuda onion, minced | 18–24 thin wedges Granny Smith apples |
| 2 cloves garlic, minced | 6 tablespoons golden whitefish caviar |
| 1 egg | |

1. Combine veal, lemon juice, mustard, onion, garlic, egg, salt and pepper in a large bowl. Mix well.
2. Place two leaves of Boston lettuce on each salad plate. Then place a nicely shaped mound of the veal tartar in the center. Arrange the Pasta Salad around the mound.
3. Arrange the apples in and around the tartar and over the pasta. Place the caviar on top of the tartar mound and serve.

## Lexander

### PASTA SALAD

- 1 pound curly-Q pasta, cooked, chilled
- 2 medium-size red peppers, seeded, julienned
- ⅓ cup small capers
- 6 scallions, cut into 2" pieces
- 6 artichoke hearts, quartered
- ¼ cup almonds, toasted

Toss pasta, peppers, capers, scallions, artichoke hearts and almonds with the dressing.

### PASTA SALAD DRESSING

- 3 lemons, juice only
- 6 cloves garlic, minced
- 1 cup olive oil
- Salt and freshly ground black pepper

1. Combine lemon juice and garlic in a bowl.
2. Whisk in the olive oil in a thin steady stream. Season with salt and pepper.

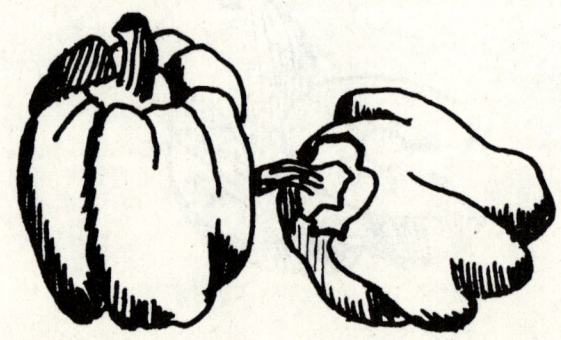

## Lexander
### CREAM of CHILI SOUP

| | |
|---|---|
| 1¼ pound veal or beef chuck eye, ground | 1 bell pepper, diced |
| ½ cup olive oil | 1 cup tomato paste |
| 5 cloves garlic, crushed | 1 cup ESPAÑOL SAUCE |
| 2 medium-size Bermuda onions, diced | 4 to 6 teaspoon chili powder |
| 3 ribs celery, diced | 1 tablespoon cayenne pepper |
| 3 carrots, peeled, diced | 1 quart whipping cream |

1. Sauté the meat in a heavy skillet with ¼ cup of the oil.
2. Sauté at the same time but in a separate skillet the garlic, onion, celery, carrots, pepper in a ¼ cup of the oil. Do not brown the vegetables.
3. Combine the meat and the vegetables, tomato paste and Español Sauce in a saucepan. Bring to a boil, reduce heat and simmer for about 30 minutes.
4. Add chili powder, cayenne and cream. Cook until heated through.
5. Season with salt to taste. Serve garnished with sour cream or chives.

*There are over one hundred varieties of chiles in Mexico alone, and all of these cross-polinate easily.*

# LEXANDER

### ESPAÑOL SAUCE

4 tablespoons butter
1 tablespoon olive oil
1 onion, diced
1 large carrot, sliced
3 ribs celery, sliced
1 cup mushrooms, sliced
2 tablespoons flour

1 large tomato, sliced
2 tablespoons tomato paste
1½ cups chicken stock
5 to 6 tablespoons dry sherry
Salt and pepper
1 bay leaf

1. Heat the butter and oil in a 3- to 4-quart saucepan. Sauté the onion, carrot and celery until soft. Add mushroom and continue cooking until they are soft.
2. Sprinkle flour over vegetables and continue cooking until vegetables are brown. Stir continuously.
3. Mix in tomato, tomato paste, chicken stock, sherry, salt, pepper and bay leaf. Bring mixture to a boil, reduce and simmer for 35 to 40 minutes. Strain. Makes about 1¼ to 1½ cups sauce.

## Lexander

### ROAST FILLET of PEPPERED PORK with BRANDY SAUCE

   3  (8 ounce) fillets of pork  
  ¾  cup black peppercorns,  
      freshly crushed  

   3  tablespoons butter  
      BRANDY CREAM SAUCE

1. Preheat oven to 350°.
2. Roll the fillets of pork in freshly crushed peppercorns. Refrigerate for 2 hours.
3. Heat butter in a large heavy skillet until it is extremely hot. Brown the fillets on all sides. Place pork in a roasting pan and place in oven. Cook until medium, about 10 minutes. Remove from pan and slice on a serving plate. Lace Sauce around pork and serve hot.

# Lexander

### BRANDY CREAM SAUCE

   8  *shallots, chopped*
   1  *bunch fresh mint, chopped*
   2  *cups dry white wine*
   2  *cups cream*
   2  *cups brown sauce or*
       *ESPAÑOL SAUCE*
1½  *cups brandy*
 ½  *lemon, juice only*

1. Reduce the shallots, mint and white wine in a saucepan to 4 tablespoons. Add cream and reduce by half. Add the brown sauce and reduce by one-third.
2. Place brandy in a separate saucepan over a high flame. Flame it. Add to the sauce. Strain through a fine sieve; season with salt and lemon juice.

*Roasted meat just removed from the oven should have sauce on the side, not the top so as to preserve the exterior crunch and show off the robust interior color.*

## LEXANDER

### CHINESE CABBAGE SALAD

| | |
|---|---|
| 1 head Chinese cabbage, cut into bite-size pieces | 2 ounces fresh feta cheese, grated |
| 12 to 15 snow peas, julienned | BUTTERMILK DRESSING |
| 2 large tomatoes, seeded, julienned | |

To assemble salad, arrange cabbage onto 6 individual serving plates. Place peas and tomatoes on top. Sprinkle with cheese. Ladle dressing over salad and serve.

### BUTTERMILK DRESSING

| | |
|---|---|
| 1 cup buttermilk | 1 tablespoon parsley, chopped |
| ½ cup sour cream | Salt and white pepper |

Combine all the ingredients in a jar, cover and shake until all are thoroughly blended. Refrigerate until needed.

*Chinese cabbage or bok choy is a tender, delicate vegetable with long smooth white stems and large dark green leaves. It has a clear light taste. Available year round, it can also be stir-fried with meat or poultry. It will keep up to a week.*

## LEXANDER

### BANANA SPLIT MERINGUE

MERINGUE
6 Maraschino cherries
⅓ cup Kirschwasser
1 cup heavy whipping cream
4 tablespoons sugar

6 bananas, peeled, sliced lengthwise
CARAMEL SAUCE
6 tablespoons chopped hazelnuts, toasted

1. Place Meringue in center of a plate. Soak cherries in Kirschwasser.
2. Whip heavy cream until soft peaks form. Add sugar and continue beating until stiff peaks form. Spread length of Meringue with whipped cream.
3. Cover with a split banana. Top with Caramel Sauce. Sprinkle with hazelnuts.
4. Place a dollop of whipped cream on top and garnish with a Maraschino cherry.

# Lexander

### MERINGUE

½ cup egg whites, about 4 whites       1 cup sugar

1. Preheat oven to 250°.
2. Beat egg whites until soft peaks form. Steadily add sugar and continue beating until stiff peaks form. Place egg white meringue in a pastry bag fitted with a straight tube.
3. Line a sheet pan with lightly greased parchment paper. Draw the shape of a banana, 1 inch by 5 inches, six times on the paper. Pipe the meringue onto the banana shapes.
4. Place in oven for about 1 hour or until tan-colored. Turn off oven and open door. Allow meringues to cool for another hour in the open oven.

### CARAMEL SAUCE

4 tablespoons unsalted butter, softened       1¼ cups sugar
1½ to 2 cups cream

1. Cook butter and sugar on a high flame in a heavy small saucepan until brown and bubbling. It should begin to caramelize.
2. Whisk in the cream in a slow steady stream until you reach desired sauce consistency.

*Eggs for meringue should be at room temperature and the utensils should be dry and free from any grease. Meringues are one of those wonderful concoctions and are the basis for many great treats such as vacherins, cookies, pie toppings and baked Alaska.*

# MESÓN del Lago

*Dinner for Six*

*Seviche*

*Orange Salad*

*Black Bean Soup*

*Chile Rellenos con Queso*

*Flan*

*Beverage:*

*Carta Blanca (Mexican beer)*

*James O. Restrepo, Manager*

*Don Rubino, Chef*

## Meson del Lago

Open since 1974, Meson del Lago is a handsome Mexican restaurant situated east of Michigan Avenue on Ontario Avenue. Manager Jimmy Restrepo proudly relates how the decorating process included a motor trip to Mexico City, where he found fragile hand-made tiles, sconces and hand-painted wash basins. The feel of Meson del Lago is that of a restaurant in La Zona Rosa, the heart of Mexico City.

Chef Don Rubino trained in Mexico City and then in the United States. He has been with Meson del Lago since the opening. "Our menu is primarily foods from the capital area around Mexico City." But he adds, "We will provided a special menu for private parties."

The special attraction of the Meson del Lago is the exciting Taco Bar situated at the rear of the restaurant. It features twenty items, both hot and cold. The hot food includes tacos, tostados, enchiladas, tamales, chicken, rice and beans, while the cold food items include toppings for the tacos such as sour cream, vegetables, guacamole and as many as six salads.

The food at Meson del Lago is both authentic and varied. The same careful consideration is given to the cuisine as was given to the decor.

158 East Ontario Avenue

## Meson del Lago

### SEVICHE

- 1 pound very fresh scallops
- ¾ cup freshly squeezed lime juice, about 6 limes
- 1 medium onion, thinly sliced
- 1 (3½ ounce) can green chiles, drained, seeded, chopped
- 1 large tomato, diced
- 4 tablespoons virgin olive oil
- ½ teaspoon oregano
- ½ teaspoon salt
- ½ cup fresh cilantro

1. Slice scallops into ½-inch slices. Place in a glass bowl and toss with the lime juice. Mix in sliced onion. Cover and allow scallops to marinate, refrigerated, overnight. Toss occasionally. They should turn opaque.
2. Drain off excess liquid. Stir in chiles, tomato, olive oil and oregano. Season to taste with salt. Serve garnished with cilantro.

*This interesting blend of ingredients obtains its flavor from the freshly squeezed lime juice.*

## Meson del Lago

### ORANGE SALAD

- 6 large oranges
- 2 medium-size red onions
- Crisp lettuce leaves
- ORANGE SALAD DRESSING
- ½ cup pitted black olives, sliced

1. Peel and thinly slice the oranges. Place in a glass bowl.
2. Thinly slice onions and toss with oranges.
3. Toss onions and oranges with Orange Salad Dressing. Cover and refrigerate for 2 hours.
4. Wash and dry the lettuce leaves. Tear into bite-size pieces. Arrange lettuce on chilled salad plates. Place orange salad on lettuce and garnish with black olives.

### ORANGE SALAD DRESSING

- ¼ cup olive oil
- ¼ cup red wine vinegar
- ½ teaspoon salt
- ½ teaspoon white pepper

Combine all ingredients and reserve until needed.

## Meson del Lago

### BLACK BEAN SOUP

| | |
|---|---|
| 1 pound black beans | ¼ cup olive oil |
| ¼ pound bacon | 2 cloves garlic, minced |
| 2 quarts BEEF STOCK | 1 large onion, diced |
| 1 smoked pork hock, cracked | 1 leek, sliced |
| 1 bay leaf | 1 carrot, diced |
| 1 teaspoon oregano | ¼ cup Madeira |
| 1 teaspoon cumin | |

1. Wash beans, and soak overnight covered with water. Drain and discard any foreign matter.
2. Sauté bacon in a 5-quart saucepan. Crumble bacon when cool enough. Discard all but 4 tablespoons of drippings. Add Beef Stock, black beans, pork hock, bay leaf, oregano and cumin.
3. Heat olive oil in a large skillet. Sauté garlic, onion, leek, carrot and celery until vegetables are limp. Add to beef stock.
4. Cover and simmer 1 hour or until beans are soft. Discard bay leaf. Remove hock and reserve.
5. Blend or process beans until smooth. Return beans to soup stock. Dice ham from hock and return to soup. Salt as necessary. Stir in Madeira. Reheat and serve hot.

### BEEF STOCK

| | |
|---|---|
| 3 pounds beef shank bones, split | 1 carrot, coarsely chopped |
| 1 large onion, chopped | 2 bay leaves |
| ¼ pound celery, sliced | ½ teaspoon each salt and pepper |

1. Boil all ingredients in a large stock pot, covered with water. Reduce heat to simmer and cook for 1½ to 2 hours covered.
2. Skim off any scum or fat as it rises to the surface. Strain the stock. Refrigerate until ready to use.

*Red kidney beans, pinto beans and the black beans are readily obtainable in most supermarkets. Beans range in color from white, pink and yellow to dark red and black. Beans are served at almost every meal in Mexico.*

## Meson del Lago

### CHILE RELLENOS con QUESO

6 poblano peppers
1½ pounds Mozzarella cheese, shredded
¼ cup lard
1 onion, sliced thin
4 tablespoons flour
1½ pounds tomatoes, pureed
2 cloves garlic, minced
1 teaspoon oregano
½ teaspoon cumin
2 bay leaves
2 cups CHICKEN STOCK
4 eggs, separated
Flour for coating
2 cups vegetable oil

1. Broil poblano peppers until blistered. Peel and remove seeds. Stuff with cheese. Place on a cookie sheet and freeze.
2. Heat lard in a skillet, add onion and sauté until soft. Add 2 tablespoons flour and whisk for 1 minute to prevent lumping. Add tomato puree, garlic, oregano, cumin, bay leaves and Chicken Stock. Simmer 15 to 20 minutes, stirring occasionally.
3. In a large bowl beat the egg whites until stiff but not dry. Whisk together egg yolks and 2 tablespoons flour. Gently fold yolks into whites.
4. Flour frozen chiles and coat with egg mixture.
5. Heat oil to 375°. Fry chiles, 4 or 5 at a time, until brown, turning once. Remove with slotted spoon and drain on toweling.
6. Arrange rellenos on serving plate and ladle heated tomato sauce over them. Serve hot.

*If poblano peppers are unavailable, substitute red or green bell peppers.*

### CHICKEN STOCK

5 to 6 pound chicken, cut in pieces
¼ pound celery, sliced
3 carrots, sliced
4 to 5 sprigs parsley
2 teaspoons salt
½ teaspoon white pepper

## Meson del Lago

1. Place all ingredients except salt and pepper in an 8-quart pot. Add cold water to cover. Bring to a boil over medium-high heat.
2. Skim off fat that rises to top. Add salt and pepper, cover. Reduce heat and simmer for 2½ hours.
3. Remove chicken pieces. Strain stock through 2 layers of cheesecloth. Cool stock. Refrigerate until needed. Makes about 6 cups.

### FLAN

*1½ cups sugar*
*1 quart milk or half and half*
*1 teaspoon vanilla extract*
*1 teaspoon rum flavoring*
*4 eggs*
*6 egg yolks*

1. Preheat oven to 350°.
2. Melt 1 cup of sugar in heavy saucepan over high heat to caramelize. Stir constantly with a wooden spoon. Immediately pour carmelized sugar into bottom of 6 to 8 individual flan molds. Quickly turn and tip from side to side so as to coat bottoms of molds evenly.
3. Scald milk with ½ cup of sugar, vanilla and rum flavorings. Allow to cool. Beat together the eggs and egg yolks. Add eggs slowly to cooled milk mixture. Strain. Pour over the caramel layer in the molds.
4. Set molds in roasting pan. Fill pan with hot water to half the height of the molds. Bake flan in oven for 1 hour or until an inserted knife comes out clean. Remove from oven and cool. Chill until ready to serve.
5. To serve, run knife around edge of mold to loosen flan. Invert on a plate.

*A 1½-quart mold can be substituted for the individual molds.*

Dinner for Six

Soft Shell Crabs with Lemon Butter Sauce

Clam Chowder

Mahi Mahi Amandine

Carrots à la Ricci

Lucien Cream

Wine:

A White Alsatian Wine

Nick Nickolas and Jeff Harman, Owners

Aaron Placourakis, General Manager

Robert DeCinzo, Executive Chef

# Nick's Fishmarket

The walls of the restaurant are a combination of natural woods, sculptured stucco surfaces and mirrored expanses. Some four dozen oil paintings by Hawaiian artist John Young decorate the dining rooms, and a dozen of LeRoy Neiman's sports-oriented works adorn the lounge. There is a mirror-walled dance floor next to the bar. No trace of fishnets or other aquatic gewgaws are to be found. Guests are seated in four-foot-high upholstered private booths, each equipped with its own dimmer switch and a telephone jack.

The menu at Nick's Fishmarket centers around seafood, including rarely found abalone, mahi-mahi and catfish. There is a choice of veal, chicken and beef dishes as well. Desserts include chocolate and amaretto mousse pies, ice creams, New York style cheesecake and a fresh papaya filled with ice cream and topped with fresh strawberries.

Nick's opened in the Loop at the end of 1977. A new edition opened in downtown Houston in 1981. Complimentary appetizers are served during weekday cocktail hours.

One First National Bank Plaza, Monroe and Dearborn Streets

# Nick's Fishmarket

## SOFT SHELL CRABS with LEMON BUTTER SAUCE

8 large soft shell crabs
Flour
4 ounces vegetable oil

LEMON BUTTER SAUCE
2 lemons, halved

1. Rinse crabs and pat dry with a paper towel. Dust crabs with flour.
2. Heat oil in a large iron skillet. Place crabs, underside down, in the hot oil. Sauté 4 to 5 minutes per side.
3. Place crabs on warmed plates and top with Lemon Butter Sauce.
4. Garnish with lemon wheel on top of crabs, lemon halves on side.

### LEMON BUTTER SAUCE

4 tablespoons butter
2 lemons, juice only

Parsley, chopped

Heat butter in saucepan, add lemon juice and chopped parsley. Stir to combine.

*To clean crabs, turn them on their backs and lift up the apron. Remove the apron by lifting the flap at each end and pulling out the spongy gill tissue. Remove eyes with scissors. Press down above legs and remove the bile sac.*

## NICK'S FISHMARKET

### CLAM CHOWDER

- ¾ pound bacon, diced
- 1 medium-size onion, diced
- 1 cup diced celery
- 1 cup diced leek, green part only
- 1 (16 ounce) can tomatoes, drained, diced
- 4 (10 ounce) cans chopped clams
- 5 (8 ounce) bottles clam juice
- 3 cups water
- ¼ cup vegetable oil
- ⅓ cup flour
- 1¾ cup half and half
- 3 medium-size Russet potatoes, peeled, diced, cooked
- Salt and pepper
- Thyme

1. Cook bacon until crisp in large stock pot. Add onion, celery, leek, tomato and stir-fry for 2 to 3 minutes.
2. Add clams, clam juice and water. Bring to a boil.
3. Heat oil in a saucepan. Slowly stir in flour until it is smooth.
4. Add this flour roux to pot, stirring constantly. Add half and half and cooked potatoes. Season with salt, pepper and thyme.

*If recipe is prepared in advance, do not precook potatoes as they will cook sufficiently during cooking and reheating.*

## Nick's Fishmarket

### MAHI MAHI AMANDINE

  8 (4 ounce) fillets of Mahi Mahi
  Flour
  ¾ cup vegetable oil
  8 tablespoons butter, browned
  4 ounces almonds, sliced, blanched

1. Dust each fillet with flour. Sauté fish in vegetable oil that has been heated to about 350°; approximately 4 minutes per side.
2. Place two fillets on each plate and top with butter and almonds.

## NICK'S FISHMARKET

### CARROTS à la RICCI

1 pound fresh carrots
Flour
3 eggs, slightly beaten
¾ cup vegetable oil

6 tablespoons butter, browned
6 ounces almonds, sliced, blanched

1. Wash and thinly slice carrots at an angle.
2. Dust carrots with flour and dip in egg wash.
3. Sauté carrots in hot vegetable oil about 1 minute or until golden brown.
4. Top carrots with butter and almonds to serve.

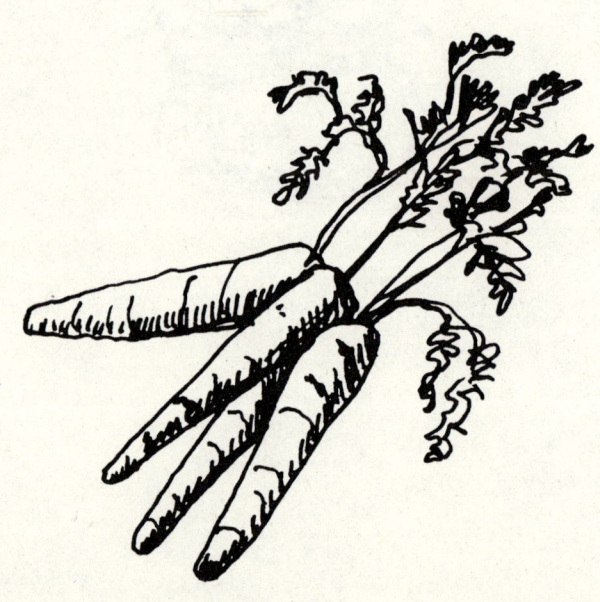

## NICK'S FISHMARKET

### LUCIAN CREAM

1¼ cup sugar
¾ cup water
1¼ tablespoons clear gelatin, softened

1½ cups heavy whipping cream
2½ cups sour cream
1½ teaspoons vanilla extract
½ teaspoon rosewater

1. Bring sugar and water to a boil in a medium-size saucepan. Turn heat down to simmer and whisk in softened gelatin.
2. Mix together whipping cream, sour cream, vanilla and rosewater in a large bowl.
3. Stir sugar water mixture into the cream mixture.
4. Pour into molds and refrigerate for at least 2 hours.
5. Unmold to serve and top with fresh seasonal berries.

*Rosewater is a delightful middle-eastern essence. It is the perfume-like waters that are distilled from rose petals of the pink damask rose. Most Gourmet food stores will carry it.*

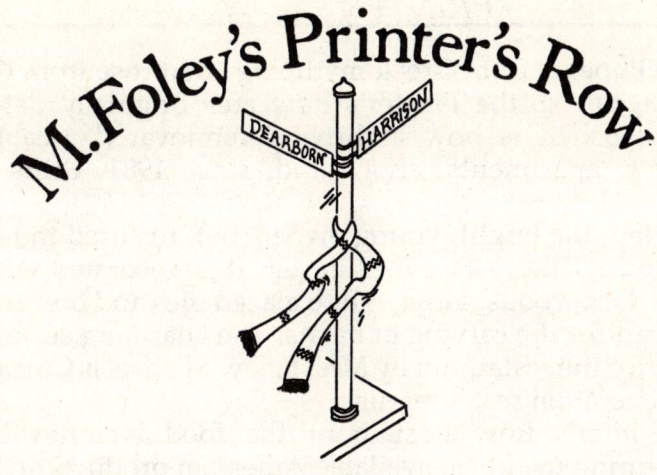

# M. Foley's Printer's Row

*Dinner for Six*

*Vegetable Ravioli with Tomato Butter*

*Medallions of Veal with Ginger and Lime*

*Sautéed Vegetables*

*Orange Custard with Fresh Fruit*

*Wine:*

*California Chardonnay*

*Michael Foley, Owner/Chef*

## Printer's Row

Like the Phoenix from Greek mythology that rose from the ashes to fly again, so the Printer's Row area originally destined to be demolished is now a thriving rennovated area boasting condominiums, apartments, shops and, since 1981, Printer's Row Restaurant.

Michael Foley, the bright, young owner/chef, restored the spacious area now housing the restaurant himself. It is decorated with glass, paneled with dark woods, vinyl, white glazed tiles and boasts a silver-plated roast cart for the carving of meats. The charming curtains were custom made for the restaurant by Mrs. Foley. Michael is Chicago-born and a third generation restaurateur.

Here at Printer's Row Restaurant the food is innovative and nouvelle, featuring the finest available American products and reflecting the increasing American taste for the not too heavy yet quite sophisticated.

Printer's Row offers such specialties as pâté with onion jam or corn crepes wrapped around goat cheese and finished with apples; sweetbreads with sautéed Belgian endive, green peppercorns and lime; and perfect lamb with vegetable mousse. "All of our menu items are the results of indigenous American ingredients," proudly states the menu.

550 South Dearborn Street

# Printer's Row

## VEGETABLE RAVIOLI with TOMATO BUTTER

¾ cup flour  
1 egg  
1 tablespoon water  

RAVIOLI FILLING  
TOMATO BUTTER

1. Combine flour, egg and water in the bowl of an electric mixer with a dough hook and mix well. Dough should be firm and smooth. Or mound flour on a bread board with a well in the center. Add egg and water and carefully incorporate into flour with agile fingers.
2. Divide the dough in half; cover with a damp cloth for 1 hour.
3. Roll out each half as thinly as possible and let dry for 15 minutes. Either a rectangle or square shape will do.
4. Either place the first sheet of dough on a ravioli pan, or on a floured surface and cut ravioli shapes with a 3½- to 4-inch cookie cutter.
5. Place ½ teaspoon of the Filling in the middle of each ravioli.
6. Combine 1 egg and 1 tablespoon of water to make an egg wash. Brush the dough around the Filling with the egg wash. Place the remaining sheet over the ravioli pan and press together along the brushed seams. If cutting out shapes, place a second shape on top of the Filling and press the edges together.
7. Bring a large pot of water to a boil. Slide a few ravioli at a time into the water and cook until al dente, just a couple of minutes. Drain and serve topped with Tomato Butter.

## PRINTER'S ROW

### RAVIOLI FILLING

- 2 tablespoons butter
- 2 tablespoons each:
    - finely chopped red and green pepper
    - mushrooms
    - red onion
    - carrot
    - broccoli
- ½ cup riccota cheese, drained
- 2 egg yolks
- Salt, pepper, nutmeg, to taste

1. Melt butter in a sauté pan over medium heat. Add the vegetables and cook until tender, about 5 minutes.
2. Drain vegetables well and transfer to a medium-size bowl.
3. Mix in cheese, egg yolks, salt, pepper and nutmeg. Stir well. Set aside and cool to room temperature.

### TOMATO BUTTER

- 2 tablespoons finely chopped shallots
- 3 tablespoons water
- 3 tablespoons wine vinegar
- 1 tablespoon tomato paste
- ½ pound butter
- 1 tablespoon shredded fresh basil
- ½ lemon, juice only

1. Place shallots, water, vinegar and tomato paste in a heavy saucepan. Reduce by lightly boiling until approximately 2 tablespoons remain. Stir occasionally.
2. Whisk in the butter, piece by piece.
3. Mix in basil and a few drops of lemon juice for pungency. Season to taste with salt and pepper. Serve atop ravioli.

## Printer's Row

### MEDALLIONS of VEAL with GINGER and LIME

Zest of one lime, finely chopped
1 3" piece of ginger, finely chopped
⅓ cup water
1 tablespoon sugar
6 ounces clarified butter
1½ pounds veal, cut in thin slices, lightly pounded into 4" medallions (2 per person)
1 large tomato, peeled, seeded, chopped
1½ cups heavy cream

1. Blanch lime zest in a covered, small saucepan, about 2 minutes. Drain; reserve.
2. Place ginger in a 1-quart saucepan with the water and sugar. Boil until all the water has evaporated. Reserve ginger in saucepan.
3. Heat butter in a 10- to 12-inch skillet until hot. Sauté veal for approximately 1 minute on each side. Remove veal to a heated plate when done and cover with foil.
4. Drain drippings from skillet. Add chopped tomato. Cook over medium heat, scraping all the food particles from the sides and bottom. Continue until tomatoes are dry.
5. Add cream and simmer until cream thickens. Strain into saucepan containing the ginger. Heat until warm.
6. Arrange veal medallions on a heated serving plate. Spoon sauce over veal. Garnish with blanched lime zest.

*Ginger root is a gnarled potato-like root that has a pungent, fresh, spicy taste. The young firm roots usually have the more delicate flavor. To use, lightly scrape skin away and slice or mince. It is said ginger root brings good luck.*

## SAUTÉED VEGETABLES

1 cucumber
1 large carrot
1 leek
1 zucchini

1 pound mushrooms, sliced
2 tablespoons olive oil
Salt and dried red pepper flakes

1. Peel and seed cucumber.
2. Peel and thinly slice carrot.
3. Separate the leek into the white and the darker green parts. Soak in water to rid it of its usual sand.
4. Do not peel zucchini. Cut all the vegetables except mushrooms into 3-inch sections. Slice each section into thin strips. Lay three or four strips together and cut each group into matchstick size. Continue until all vegetables are done so.
5. Combine and toss all the vegetables with the mushrooms.
6. Heat 2 tablespoons of oil in a 10- to 12-inch skillet. Add vegetables and sauté lightly so they are done but still crisp.
7. Season with salt and red pepper flakes.

*"Because of the nature of the rich sauce for the veal, I have chosen a simple vegetable mixture of julienne zucchini, cucumber, carrot, leek and sliced mushrooms. The nature of the cuts is to keep all the vegetables as crisp as possible during cooking time. If cut as directed it will not be necessary to blanch them."—Michael Foley*

# Printer's Row

## ORANGE CUSTARD with FRESH FRUIT

8 egg yolks
4 eggs
1 cup sugar
Zest of 1 orange or tangerine
¼ cup orange juice, freshly squeezed
3 cups milk
1 teaspoon vanilla

1. Preheat oven to 350°.
2. Oil a 1½-quart custard dish or pâté mold.
3. Whisk together yolks and eggs. Add sugar and beat until smooth.
4. Add grated zest. Add juice, beat for 1 minute. Eggs and sugar should be pale in color and thick.
5. Bring milk to a boil in a saucepan over medium heat. Slowly pour into the egg mixture, stirring constantly. Add vanilla.
6. Pour into oiled mold and place mold in roasting pan of water. Place in oven and cook until inserted knife comes out clean, about 45 minutes. Refrigerate until cool.
7. Serve with seasonal fruits.

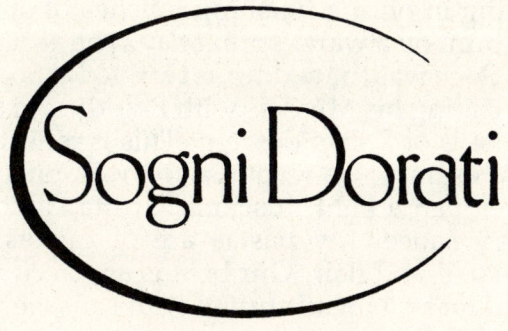

*Dinner for Four*

*Veal-Stuffed Apples*

*Pasta Salad*

*Sogni Dorati's Duck with Chianti and Rosemary Sauce*

*Anise Carrots*

*Ricotta Cheese Cake*

*Wine:*

*Chianti Classico Conte Capponi 1977*

*Silvio Pinto, Owner/Chef*

## Sogni Dorati

Imagine walking in on the finishing touches of an Italian cooking class about 5 p.m. on a warm spring day. The aroma is truly nectar for the Gods. Such was the setting as I arrived at Sogni Dorati; Silvio Pinto was just finishing his Mussels with Brandy and Saffron. "I'm an American chef that is of Italian descent. This is reflected in my recipe development. For example, in response to the popularity of the flourless cakes, I developed a light, luscious Ricotta Almond Cheesecake with a strawberry sauce. My pastas are of carrots, tomatoes and spinach, adding color and flair. Our breads are laced with escarole or perhaps we might make a bread stuffed with sausage."

The restaurant this day was empty except for the long mahogany bar that sits opposite the balcony room. The bar is dominated by an imported espresso machine. "My brother, the one that is the architect, and I designed the restaurant and the kitchen," said Silvio. The restaurant is decorated with Art Deco overtones and antiques representing the artistic life of the owner. The balcony has a player piano on one end providing entertainment.

This family-owned and -operated restaurant is a symphony of co-operation. The pastry and bread is created by a cousin and Mama de Pinto is ever present in the kitchen. Today she was just finishing some breads for the nursing home. Sister Mary is in charge of the restaurant's operation. Silvio is responsible for recipe development, teaching and the kitchen.

Sogni Dorati means golden dreams, and as such represents the dreams of the immigrant family Pinto. You indeed feel lucky to have been invited to their home for dinner.

660 North Wells

## Sogni Dorati

### VEAL-STUFFED APPLES

- 6 apples, peeled, cored
- 6 tablespoons lemon juice, freshly squeezed
- ½ pound veal, ground
- ⅛ teaspoon salt
- Pinch of black pepper
- 1 rib celery, minced
- 2 sprigs parsley, minced
- 1 tablespoon Parmesan cheese, grated
- ½ cup raisins
- ¼ teaspoon sage
- ¼ cup bread crumbs
- ½ cup walnuts, chopped
- 1 egg, slightly beaten
- 1 cup VEAL STOCK
- 1 tablespoon honey
- 1 tablespoon apple brandy
- 4 tablespoons butter, melted
- 6 sprigs parsley

1. Preheat oven to 350°.
2. Rub apples with lemon juice.
3. Place veal, salt, pepper, celery, parsley, cheese, raisins, sage, crumbs, walnuts and egg in a large mixing bowl and combine.
4. Stuff core of apples with veal mixture and arrange in baking dish.
5. Combine Veal Stock, honey, apple brandy and butter. Drizzle over apples.
6. Bake apples 20 minutes or until soft. Garnish with parsley, serve hot.

*Pine nuts may be substituted for the walnuts. They are the kernel of pine cones and resemble almonds somewhat in taste.*

## Sogni Dorati

### VEAL STOCK

- 2½ pounds veal knuckles, cut in 2" pieces
- 1 large onion, quartered
- 2 leeks, washed, cut into 2" pieces
- 2 carrots, sliced
- 2 ribs celery, sliced
- 3 sprigs parsley

1. Cover veal bones with water in a large stock pot and bring to a boil. Add remaining ingredients. Simmer for 2 hours.
2. Skim any foam that may arise to the surface. Strain stock through cheesecloth. Chill until needed.

# Sogni Dorati

## PASTA SALAD

1 large bunch broccoli
1 pound pasta shells
⅛ cup oil
2 cloves garlic, minced
¼ teaspoon red pepper

1 slice ginger, peeled, minced
Zest of 1 orange
Juice of 1 orange
½ cup of water
Salt and pepper, to taste

1. Wash broccoli. Cut small florets from stems. Peel and slice stem. Blanch stems and florets in lightly salted boiling water until color turns bright green. Place in cold water until they have cooled off. Drain.
2. Boil pasta al dente. Drain.
3. Heat oil in small skillet, add garlic. Sauté until garlic turns white. Add red pepper, ginger, zest, juice and water. Simmer for 2 to 3 minutes, stirring occasionally.
4. Toss pasta and broccoli with sauce. Season with salt and pepper.

## Sogni Dorati

### SOGNI DORATI'S DUCK with CHIANTI and ROSEMARY SAUCE

1 (5–6 pound) duck
½ cup chopped celery
½ cup chopped onion
½ cup chopped carrot

Unsalted butter
CHIANTI AND
ROSEMARY SAUCE

1. Preheat oven to 350°.
2. Remove giblets and rinse duck, inside and out. Remove breast skin and cut duck breast from bone, creating two half-breast pieces. Remove legs and thigh as one piece without removing skin.
3. Sauté the liver gently in several tablespoons of butter and reserve. Cut in thin slices and use as garnish.
4. Sauté all bones in a large pot, including wings and remaining giblets in several tablespoons of butter. Add celery, onion and carrot. Cover with several quarts of water and bring to a boil; reduce heat and simmer for 3 to 4 hours. Cool, then skim off fat. Strain. Reheat stock and reduce by half.
5. Cook leg and thigh pieces, skin on, in pan covered with foil in oven for 1 hour and 15 minutes. Try to time this so the duck is done as the stock finishes up.
6. For medium rare: Poach breast slowly for about 9 minutes in very hot but not simmering stock. Or sauté gently in a saucepan in butter for 8 to 10 minutes. Or grill on stove-top electric grill for 6 minutes. Serve breasts and legs with Sauce.

## Sogni Dorati

**CHIANTI and ROSEMARY SAUCE**

| | |
|---|---|
| 2 cups Duck Stock | ⅛ teaspoon salt |
| ½ cup Chianti | Pinch of black pepper |
| ¼ teaspoon dried rosemary | 5 to 6 tablespoons butter, softened |

1. Combine all ingredients except butter and reduce over high heat until sauce is reduced to about ⅓ cup.
2. Remove sauce from heat and whisk in butter until thickened.
3. Return the duck breast to the pan at the very end to give duck even more flavor.

## Sogni Dorati

### ANISE CARROTS

| | |
|---|---|
| 1 pound carrots, peeled, sliced | 6 tablespoons butter |
| 1 small onion, chopped | ½ teaspoon anise, crushed |
| | 5 to 6 tablespoons orange juice |

1. Cook carrots in salted water until tender. Drain.
2. Sauté onion in 2 tablespoons of butter until soft.
3. Return carrots to saucepan. Add remaining butter, anise and orange juice. Season with salt and pepper.
4. Cook over medium heat until butter has melted and ingredients have blended. Stir occasionally. Serve hot.

## Sogni Dorati

### RICOTTA CHEESECAKE

3 pounds Ricotta cheese, drained
5 eggs
½ cup sugar
⅛ teaspoon salt
2 tablespoons flour
½ teaspoon almond extract

1. Preheat oven to 350°.
2. Use a food processor fitted with a steel blade. Place half of each of the ingredients in the bowl and process until smooth.
3. Mound this batch into a greased loaf pan. Repeat process with remaining portion of the ingredients and add to the loal pan.
4. Bake 45 minutes or until the cake is spongy to the touch. Cool and unmold. Slice and serve.

*Ricotta is a fresh, moist, unsalted variety of cottage cheese. It is used in salads, lasagna and blintzes as well as in desserts.*

*Dinner for Six*

*Alaskan Salmon Steak Tartar*

*Salad Mimosa*

*Croustade of Bay Scallops
with Saffron and Julienne Vegetables*

*Chocolate Silken Torte*

*Wine:*

*With Tartar, Perrier-Jouet Grand Brut*

*With Croustade, 1979 Chassagne Montrachet*

*With Dessert, Cognac or Grand Marnier*

*George Badonsky, Owner*

*Henri Coudrier, Chef*

*Elliot Baron, Manager*

## Tango

The recently refurbished Tango restaurant is decorated with primitive African works, original lithographs and paintings by Salvador Dali, Ed Paschke and Andy Warhol. Dining at Tango is like eating in a modern art museum. A twelve-member group of the Chicago City Ballet performed at the reopening of Tango to help in the celebration.

The soft peach and gray colors are balanced by the warmth of the Brauer chairs and soft velvets. Fine china and fresh flowers adorn the tables, maintaining the intimate appeal of the restaurant.

The kitchen is tenderly watched over by the French chef Henri Coudrier. He has long been famous in the Chicago area for his creative abilities. Much of the seafood at Tango is grilled on mesquite, a hardwood from the southwest. A full gamut of seafood, from grilled red snapper to a mousse of bay scallops with an herb sauce can be found on the menu.

This classic seafood restaurant offers comfortable surroundings and wonderful food. "At Tango the meal is as sophisticated as the diner wants it to be," says Elliot Baron, Tango manager. "Here there is no pretense, just outstanding food."

Hotel Belmont, 3172 North Sheridan Road

# TANGO

## ALASKAN SALMON STEAK TARTAR

16 to 20 ounces of fresh salmon, boned and skinned
3 teaspoons capers, chopped
3 teaspoons finely chopped white onion
3 eggs, hard boiled, separated and chopped finely
3 teaspoons chopped parsley
3 anchovy fillets, chopped

Tabasco sauce
Worcestershire sauce
Freshly squeezed lemon juice
Salt and pepper
Dash of white vinegar
Garnish: black olives, cornichons, capers, chopped onion

1. Put salmon piece by piece in food processor fitted with steel blade. Process in short burst to prevent salmon from becoming too fine. Transfer to a mixing bowl.
2. Mix capers, onion, egg yolk, parsley and anchovy into salmon with a spatula. Fold carefully. Season with Tabasco, Worcestershire, lemon juice, salt, pepper and vinegar.
3. Serve in a white ceramic ramekin. Place in center of a chilled salad plate.
4. Garnish with black olives, cornichons, capers and chopped onion.

## Tango

### SALAD MIMOSA

6 heads Boston lettuce
2 teaspoons Dijon mustard
2 to 3 tablespoons white wine vinegar
¼ cup peanut oil
Salt and pepper to taste
2 teaspoons chopped chervil
2 hard boiled eggs, separated and chopped
Minced parsley

1. Wash Boston lettuce, shake out all water. Core each head and open leaves somewhat. Set aside.
2. Whisk together mustard and vinegar in a mixing bowl. Slowly drizzle in oil while whisking. Add salt and pepper to taste. Add chopped chervil.
3. Place a small amount of dressing in a bowl. Turn each head several times in the bowl before placing on a chilled salad plate. Replenish dressing in turning bowl as needed.
4. Sprinkle each head with chopped egg and parsley.

# Tango

## CROUSTADE of BAY SCALLOPS with SAFFRON and JULIENNE VEGETABLES

- 1 thin, young leek
- 1 medium-size carrot
- 1 celery stalk
- ½ cup dry white wine
- ½ cup white wine vinegar
- Juice from 1 lemon
- Pinch of saffron
- 1 tablespoon chopped shallot
- Salt and cayenne pepper
- 2 pounds bay scallops
- 1 teaspoon chopped chervil
- 5 tablespoons heavy cream
- 8 ounces butter
- 6 pastry shells

1. Trim and clean the leek. Use only the white part; split in half lengthwise. Wash carefully. Cut into 1½-inch-long strips. Also cut carrot and celery into 1½-inch-long strips.
2. Pour wine, vinegar, juice, saffron, shallot, salt and pepper into a steamer. Bring to a boil. In the top of the steamer arrange scallops, vegetables and chervil. Cover and steam for 10 minutes. At 5 minutes turn with a spatula. Remove steamer insert with scallops; keep covered and warm.
3. Add cream to the cooking juice and reduce liquid to a couple of tablespoons. Add the butter in small amounts, using a whisk. Do not bring to a boil. Pour completed sauce over the scallops. Sprinkle with parsley.
4. Serve in pastry shells. Arrange vegetables in the bottom and fill with scallops and top with sauce. Or experiment with your own presentation.

## TANGO

### CHOCOLATE SILKEN TORTE

- 1 pound semi-sweet chocolate
- 4 tablespoons butter
- 1 teaspoon instant coffee
- 2 egg yolks
- 3 tablespoons praline paste
- 2 ounces Grand Marnier
- 2½ cups heavy cream
- 2 egg whites
- 2 tablespoons sugar
- 2 cups chocolate cake crumbs
- CHOCOLATE FROSTING

1. Melt butter and chocolate in top of double boiler.
2. Combine coffee, egg yolks, praline paste and Grand Marnier in a bowl and mix well. Add melted chocolate.
3. Whip cream until stiff peaks form and fold into mixture.
4. Beat egg whites until stiff peaks form. Add sugar and continue beating. Fold into mixture.
5. Line bottom of a 10-inch springform pan with chocolate cake crumbs. Fill with chocolate mixture and chill for 24 hours.
6. Remove from springform pan and frost with Chocolate Frosting.

# Tango

### CHOCOLATE FROSTING

1 pound semi-sweet chocolate

½ pound butter

1. Melt chocolate and butter in top of a double boiler over warm water.
2. Remove from heat; blend well.

*Semi-sweet chocolate is sometimes called sweet chocolate and is the choice of French chefs for baking.*

# 三喜大酒樓
## THREE HAPPINESS

Dim Sum Brunch for Four

Spareribs with Black Bean Sauce

Har Gow

Open Steamed Dumplings

Sesame Cookies


Wine:

Wan Fu


Moy Family, Owners

## Three Happiness

Our favorite Sunday morning treat is to venture to the Chinatown's Three Happiness. That is the time of the day for Dim Sum Brunch. It is served daily in the orient but also in Chicago at the Three Happiness it is served each morning from 10 a.m. to 2 p.m. This Hong Kong tradition is becoming so popular that it is best to arrive early to avoid lengthy waits.

Dim Sum means Heart's Delight. The phrase is in loving reference to the finger foods, to the delicious bite-size morsels of meat or fish, stuffed dumplings and savory meat, marinated food, succulent sauces, noodle dishes, pan-fried delicacies—all served steaming from rolling wagons with waiters eager to help you plan your meal. This tableside presentation is both unique to this area and a delightful culinary experience.

Three Happiness is located at the entrance to Chinatown. This large, 300-seat restaurant has a full bilingual menu describing its distinctive Cantonese foods and Dim Sum Brunch. The full bar features colorful tropical drinks. The Three Happiness is the newest member of the Moy family of restaurants.

2130 South Wentworth Avenue

## Three Happiness

### SPARERIBS with BLACK BEAN SAUCE

1 pound pork spareribs
1 teaspoon minced ginger
2 teaspoons black bean paste
2 cloves garlic, minced
½ teaspoon salt
1 teaspoon sugar
1 teaspoon wine

1 teaspoon light soy sauce
Dash of pepper and sesame oil
1 teaspoon cornstarch
2 tablespoons water
1 tablespoon oil
2 green onions, minced

1. Wash ribs, cut into 1-inch pieces and place in a large mixing bowl. Stir in ginger, black bean paste and garlic. Mix well.
2. Place salt, sugar, wine, soy, oil, pepper and cornstarch in a small bowl. Add 2 tablespoons water, stir until mixed. Add oil to bind. Pour onto ribs.
3. Place ribs on a platter. Cook over hot water in a steamer for 12 minutes. Remove and scatter green onions on top. Serve hot.

*Black bean sauce is a thick, pungent puree sauce. It can be found in Oriental food stores. Once opened, it can be kept refrigerated for quite a while.*

# THREE HAPPINESS

## HAR GOW

| | |
|---|---|
| 1 cup wheat starch | Pinch of pepper |
| 2 teaspoons cornstarch | ½ teaspoon sesame oil |
| ¾ cup boiling water | 1 teaspoon cornstarch |
| 1 tablespoon lard | 1 egg white |
| ½ teaspoon salt | 10 ounces shelled shrimp |
| ½ teaspoon sugar | 2 ounces bamboo shoots |

1. For Pastry: Sift wheat starch and cornstarch into a medium size bowl and make a well in the center.
2. Pour in the boiling water, stirring rapidly. Mix in lard and knead well. Place on a lightly floured surface and knead by hand until soft.
3. Roll dough into a 1-inch diameter sausage shape. Cover and let rest for 15 minutes.
4. For Filling: Place salt, sugar, pepper, sesame oil, cornstarch and egg white in a bowl and mix well.

## Three Happiness

5. Cut each shrimp into 2 or 3 pieces. Slice or dice bamboo shoots. Add both to bowl of seasonings. Blend well. Refrigerate for 30 minutes.
6. For Assembly: Section dough into about 25 portions. Roll each portion out on a lightly floured surface into a round shape. Place a small amount, about 1 teaspoonful, of the filling on the round. Wrap dough edges up together forming a pleated bonnet shape. Seal.
7. Arrange dumplings on a greased steamer over hot water. Steam for 5 minutes. Serve hot.

*Wheat starch is wheat flour with the gluten removed. It is used to make very light, delicate translucent wrappers for Dim Sum items.*

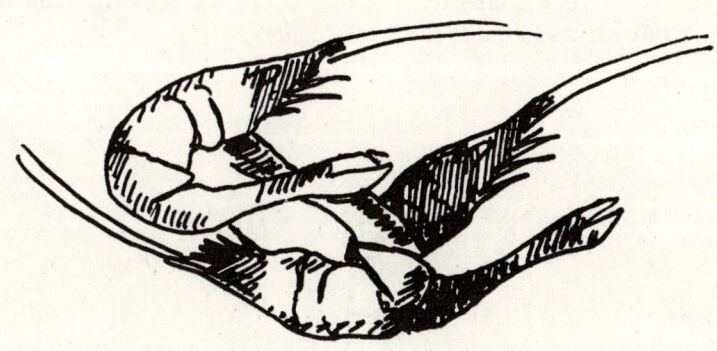

# Three Happiness

## OPEN STEAMED DUMPLINGS

- ½ pound ground pork
- 4 Chinese mushrooms, soaked in hot water for 10 minutes, minced
- 6 ounces shrimp, shelled, deveined, washed, dried, minced
- ½ teaspoon sugar
- 1 teaspoon sesame oil
- ¼ teaspoon salt
- Dash pepper
- 2 tablespoons light soy sauce
- 24 small egg roll wrappers, circle-shaped

1. Combine first eight ingredients in a medium-size bowl.
2. Place about 2 teaspoons of filling in the middle of each of the wrappers. Gather up the sides and squeeze together forming a bonnet shape. Leave the top slightly open.
3. Arrange dumplings in an oiled steamer over hot water. Steam covered for 10 to 15 minutes or until meat has cooked. Serve hot.

*A glass makes a good shape with which to cut the usually square egg roll wrappers with, so as to make them circle-shaped.*

# Three Happiness

## SESAME COOKIES

- 3 tablespoons water
- ½ cup + 2 tablespoons sugar
- 1 egg
- 1 tablespoon oil
- 1¼ cups flour
- ½ teaspoon baking powder
- ½ teaspoon baking soda
- ½ cup sesame seeds
- 2 to 3 cups oil, for frying

1. Bring water to a boil in a small saucepan and stir in sugar until dissolved.
2. Beat egg with the oil.
3. Sift flour, baking powder and baking soda. Make a well in the center. Pour in the sugar solution and the egg mixture. Slowly incorporate flour into liquid to form a soft dough. Divide into 32 portions. Shape these portions into balls.
4. Wash, drain and dry sesame seeds. Roll small balls onto seeds so as to coat evenly.
5. Bring oil to 375°. Place cookies in oil, a few at a time, and deep fry until a crack is formed on each cookie. Continue cooking until golden brown. Remove with slotted spoon and drain.

*Dinner for Four*

*Frog Legs Provençale*

*Truffles Salade Maison*

*Le Grenadin de Veau "Normade"*

*Bananas Foster*

*Wine:*

*Clos du Bois Chardonnay*

*Hyatt Regency Chicago, Owner*

*Michel Koenig, Chef*

## Truffles

Truffles is named for that elusive Perigourdine fungus, rare and delicate. The black truffle slices can be seen on most of the foods leaving Chef Michel Koenig's cavernous kitchen.

The double consommé garnished with truffles, salads of French green beans marinated and garnished with truffles, and prime tenderloin stuffed with goose liver pâté and truffles are a few examples. Only the desserts seem to be minus the fabulous fungus. Koenig, originally from Nancy, France, says "One brings with him the results of his experiences. It helps to make people unique. Therefore I really cook my own style. I don't worry about what other restaurants are doing." He carefully oversees all Truffles meal preparation.

Truffles is set in an atmosphere of casual elegance and is located on the second floor of the Hyatt Regency Chicago near Michigan Avenue on Wacker Drive. The light, bright ambiance is created by large, floor-to-ceiling glass windows, wicker baskets and luscious shades of apricot that decorate the chairs and dishes.

The French cuisine takes advantage of fresh seasonal ingredients. Truffles is the recipient of the four-star award of the Mobile Travel Guide.

Hyatt Regency Chicago, 151 East Wacker Drive

## Truffles

### FROG LEGS PROVENÇALE

12 pairs frog legs
Salt and pepper
½ cup flour
½ cup unsalted butter
1 cup mushrooms, sliced
1 cup diced tomatoes, seeded
½ cup fresh parsley, chopped
1 clove garlic, finely chopped
1 lemon, cut in wedges

1. Season frog legs with salt and pepper; then dredge in flour. Shake off the excess.
2. Heat 2 tablespoons of the butter over medium heat in a large heavy skillet. Sauté legs until golden brown, 3 to 4 minutes per side. Add butter as needed.
3. Add mushrooms, tomatoes, parsley, and garlic. Mix gently.
4. Remove legs to a warm plate. Add remaining butter to pan; heat until it starts to bubble. Pour butter and vegetables over the frog legs.
5. Garnish with lemon wedges when serving.

*The cuisine of Provence is a more highly flavored one than that of northern France. Provence has also been a favorite vacation spot for centuries.*

## Truffles

### TRUFFLES SALADE MAISON

2 small heads bibb lettuce
1 bunch watercress
2 medium size Belgian endive
1 ripe avocado
1 large tomato
WALNUT OIL DRESSING
Bleu cheese, crumbled

1. Clean lettuce: Break or cut leaves; wash in cold water; dry in paper toweling or salad spinner.
2. Wash, dry and trim watercress.
3. Cut avocados and tomatoes into eight wedges each.
4. Arrange on each plate: lettuce and watercress in center; two tomato wedges at top; three endive sections on sides; and two avocado pieces at the bottom of the plate. Drizzle with Walnut Oil Dressing and sprinkle with cheese.

## Truffles

### WALNUT OIL DRESSING

2 shallots or ½ small onion
Salt and pepper, to taste
6 tablespoons Grey Poupon mustard
1 cup walnut oil
½ cup raspberry vinegar

1. In a food processor fitted with a steel blade, and with machine running, drop shallots. Add salt and pepper and mustard.
2. In a slow steady stream, with machine still running, add the walnut oil. A mayonnaise consistency should develop.
3. Add raspberry vinegar and blend well. Chill finished dressing until needed.

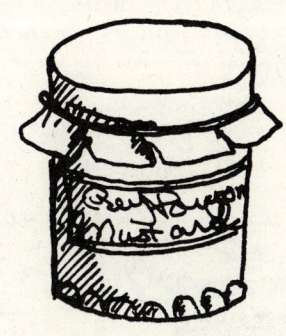

## Truffles

### LE GRENADIN DE VEAU "NORMADE"

  8  (3 ounce) veal medallions
½  cup flour
  2  tablespoons butter

  2  Washington red delicious apples, peeled, cored and cut into 8 sections
½  cup Calvados
  2  cups whipping cream

1. Dredge veal lightly with flour and shake off excess.
2. Heat 1 tablespoon butter in skillet over medium heat. Sauté veal lightly. Do not overcook. Transfer to a warm plate and keep warm. Remove grease, but retain pan for deglazing.
3. In the remaining butter sauté apples until soft, about 5 to 8 minutes.
4. Deglaze veal pan with Calvados. Quickly reduce liquid; add whipping cream and reduce until mixture thickens. Season with salt and pepper as desired.
5. Place two medallions on each plate and surround with four apple sections. Pour sauce over medallions and serve.

*Normans can boast the richest cream in all of France. Apples grow in abundance there, the majority going into the production of cider and the apple brandy Calvados.*

## Truffles

### BANANAS FOSTER

4 ripe bananas  
1 tablespoon butter  
1 tablespoon cinnamon  
½ cup brown sugar  
4 ounces Meyer's white rum  
4 scoops vanilla ice cream  

1. Peel bananas and slice lengthwise.
2. Melt butter in small skillet and sauté banana slices. Remove to a warm plate.
3. Add cinnamon and brown sugar to pan and cook over medium heat for 2 minutes or until sugar has melted. Stir constantly.
4. Add rum and cook 2 minutes longer.
5. Arrange plates with ice cream in center and bananas on the side. Spoon sauce over the ice cream and the bananas. Serve immediately.

*Dinner for Six*

*Mussel Soup*

*Grilled Rouget with Fresh Tomato Sauce
and Anchovy Butter*

*Spinach Salad with Roquefort*

*Yoshi's Fresh Pear Charlotte*

*Wine:*

*1981 Pouilly Fumé*

*Yoshi and Nobuko Katsumura, Owner/Chef*

# Yoshi's Café

Yoshi and Nobuko Katsumura have presented Chicago with the newest star in its galaxy of fine restaurants. Yoshi began his culinary training in his native Japan, primarily with the cuisine of France. He apprenticed in Europe, including Paris and Lyon. In Chicago, Yoshi developed his skill working in fine restaurants, a four-year partnership and now, Yoshi's Cafe.

The intimate cafe is a reflection of its hosts, warm and gracious. The tile floor, plum and gray coloring, and art-decorated walls provide a background for a seating of forty.

"I work hard, have nice people in my kitchen, is how I do it," says Yoshi. "Our clientele is sophisticated about food, and we respond by trying our best," he adds.

Although Yoshi's background is in the classical French cuisine his food is delightfully light and one can feel a decided Japanese flavor in the design and presentation. His creativity is felt through the entire meal. It is unpretentious excellence; a delightful eating experience.

3257 North Halstead Street

## YOSHI'S CAFÉ

### MUSSEL SOUP

2 pounds mussels
½ bottle white wine
2 shallots, chopped
2 tablespoons parsley, chopped
4 tablespoons unsalted butter
¾ cup olive oil
⅓ pound onions, minced
⅓ pound leeks, washed well and cut into strips
1½ quarts FISH STOCK

1½ pounds tomatoes, seeded and cut into pieces
1 clove garlic, chopped
½ bay leaf
1 sprig thyme
Saffron, salt and pepper, to taste
1 cup cream
1 leek, julienned
1 carrot, julienned
1 rib celery, julienned

1. Soak mussels in salted water overnight.
2. Boil the mussels with half of the wine, shallots, parsley and butter until they open. Discard any that do not open. Remove from liquid. Reserve both.
3. Heat olive oil in 8- to 10-quart stock pot. Add onions and leeks; cook over low heat for 5 minutes.
4. Pour in 4 quarts water, the remaining wine and the liquid that the mussels steamed in. Add the Fish Stock, tomatoes, garlic, bay leaf, thyme, saffron, salt and pepper. Cook for 40 minutes.
5. Put stock through a strainer. Pour into a small kettle and bring to a boil. Add the mussels and cream and cook for 2 minutes.
6. Sauté leek, carrot and celery in 3 tablespoons of butter until soft.
7. Ladle soup into soup bowls and place julienned vegetables on top of each bowl. Serve hot.

## Yoshi's Café

### FISH STOCK

1 onion, sliced
3 ribs celery, sliced
1½ cups dry white wine
2 to 2½ pounds fish bones
1½ to 2 quarts water
5 black peppercorns, crushed
1 bay leaf

Simmer all ingredients in a stock pot for approximately 45 to 50 minutes. Strain through a double layer of cheesecloth.

Brillat-Savarin said "Fish is the most inexhaustible source of culinary inspiration there is."

### GRILLED ROUGET with FRESH TOMATO SAUCE and ANCHOVY BUTTER

FRESH TOMATO SAUCE
6 (portion-size) pieces of fresh rouget, with skin
Salt and pepper, to taste
Vegetable oil
1 bunch of scallions, chopped
2 tablespoons butter
ANCHOVY BUTTER

1. Scale fish and cut into fillets. Season with salt and pepper.
2. Heat the grill until it is very hot. Brush fillets with very small amount of vegetable oil and place on the grill skin side down. Cook for 1½ minutes. Twist (not turn over) filets so as to create a criss-cross grill pattern and cook for 1½ minutes more. Turn over and cook until done, about 1½ minutes.
3. Sauté chopped scallions in butter. Season with salt and pepper.
4. Just before serving, return the Sauce to a boil in a small pan. Add remaining 2 tablespoons of butter and adjust seasonings.
5. Make a bed of scallions on plates, top with rouget fillets and place sauce around fish. Place a thin slice of Anchovy Butter on top.

## Yoshi's Café

### FRESH TOMATO SAUCE

4 tablespoons butter
1 small onion, chopped
2¼ pounds tomatoes, peeled, seeded, cut into pieces
2 cloves garlic, unpeeled

Bouquet Garni: thyme, parsley and bay leaf tied in cheesecloth
Salt, pepper, sugar, to taste

1. Melt half of butter in skillet and sauté onions, covered, for 5 minutes over low heat. Do not brown. Add remaining butter.
2. Add tomatoes, whole garlic and Bouquet Garni. Season with salt, pepper and a pinch of sugar. Cook, covered over medium heat for about 30 minutes.
3. Remove garlic and Bouquet Garni and puree the remaining sauce.

### ANCHOVY BUTTER

½ pound butter
3 ounces anchovy, grind or paste

1 pinch parsley, chopped
Dash fresh lemon juice
Dash paprika

Combine all ingredients. Place on a sheet of aluminum foil. Form a 1½- to 2-inch shape. Refrigerate for 1 hour.

## YOSHI'S CAFÉ

### SPINACH SALAD with ROQUEFORT

| | |
|---|---|
| 1 (10 ounce) bunch spinach | Dijon mustard, to taste |
| 1 ounce red wine vinegar | Salt and pepper, to taste |
| 3 ounces olive oil | Roquefort cheese, to taste crumbled |

1. Clean fresh spinach; cut stems off. Drain and dry well.
2. Take large chilled salad bowl and add vinegar, oil, mustard, salt and pepper. Mix well. Add spinach and toss.
3. Arrange neatly on a large plate and sprinkle Roquefort on top.

# YOSHI'S CAFÉ

## YOSHI'S FRESH PEAR CHARLOTTE

1 genoise, your favorite recipe or a ready-made sponge cake
2 pounds fresh pears
  Poaching syrup (equal parts sugar and water to cover pears, plus juice of one lemon to prevent pears from turning dark)
1 vanilla bean
½ ounce gelatin
8 egg yolks
4 cups sugar
1 teaspoon vanilla
1 pint milk
1 pint heavy cream

1. Make a 12-inch genoise. Cut into 3 pieces so that the middle strip is 3 inches wide. Reserve two outside pieces for another use. Slice the 3-inch strip into ½ to 1-inch slices. Line slices around a 10" cake mold. Set aside.
2. Peel fresh pears and poach in syrup with vanilla bean. Cool pears and dice.
3. Add gelatin to egg yolks with 2 cups of sugar. Whisk eggs gently and add ½ teaspoon vanilla. Mixture should not be too frothy.
4. Scale milk and slowly pour into egg mixture. Pour into heavy saucepan and reheat up to the boiling point, stirring constantly.
5. When it comes to coat a wooden spoon, remove from heat and strain. Quickly place mixture in a bowl that sits in cold water so as to stop the cooking. Continue stirring as it cools. When cool add diced pears.
6. Whip the cream, gradually adding remaining sugar and vanilla.
7. Gradually pour egg mixture into whipped cream; fold with spatula.
8. Pour mixture into cake-lined mold up to the top of the cake. Refrigerate for 1 hour.

# RECIPE INDEX

## Appetizers

Champignon Farcis, Stuffed
  Mushrooms (*Chez Paul*) . . . . . . . . . 39
Eggplant Duxelle with Roquefort
  Glaze (*Gordon*) . . . . . . . . . . . . . . . 79
Alaskan Salmon Steak
  Tartar (*Tango*) . . . . . . . . . . . . . . 155
Fried Calamari (*Chestnut Street Grill*) . . 32
Frog Legs Provençale (*Truffles*) . . . . . 171
Har Gow (*Three Happiness*) . . . . . . . . 164
Lake Tungting Smelt (*House of
  Hunan*) . . . . . . . . . . . . . . . . . . . . 96
Open Steam Dumplings (*Three
  Happiness*) . . . . . . . . . . . . . . . . . 166
Ramequin of Cray Fish
  (*L'Escargot*) . . . . . . . . . . . . . . . . . 65
Roast Goat Cheese (*Cricket's*) . . . . . . . 61
Roasted Peppers with Salami and
  Anchovies (*George's*) . . . . . . . . . . 73
Salad of Sea Scallops & Shrimp
  (*Cape Cod Room*) . . . . . . . . . . . . 23
Salmon Fingertips *The Consort*) . . . . . 49
Seviche (*Meson del Lago*) . . . . . . . . . 121
Soft Shell Crabs (*Nick's Fishmarket*) . . 129
Snails, Sweetbreads and Goat Cheese
  Ravioli (*Jovan*) . . . . . . . . . . . . . . 101
Spareribs with Black Bean Sauce
  (*Three Happiness*) . . . . . . . . . . . 163
Stockyard Inn Marinated Beef (*The
  Bakery*) . . . . . . . . . . . . . . . . . . . . 13
Veal Stuffed Apples (*Sogni Dorati*) . . . 145
Veal Tartar (*Lexander*) . . . . . . . . . . . 109
Vegetable Souffle (*Arnie's*) . . . . . . . . . 3

## Desserts

Banana Split Meringue (*Lexander*) . . . . 116
Bananas Foster (*Truffles*) . . . . . . . . . 175
Brownie Bottom Pie (*The Bakery*) . . . . 18
Crème Brûlee (*Chestnut Street Grill*) . . . 35
Chocolate Cake San Farine (*Cricket's*) . 61
Chocolate Sauce (*The Bakery*) . . . . . . . 19
Chocolate Silken Torte (*Tango*) . . . . . . 158
Chocolate Velvet Cake (*Arnie's*) . . . . . 8
Drunken Fruit Compote (*Gordon*) . . . . 85
Grand Marnier Souffle (*Jovan
  Restaurant*) . . . . . . . . . . . . . . . . 105
Linzertorte (*The Consort*) . . . . . . . . . 51
Lucian Cream (*Nick's Fishmarket*) . . . 133
Mousse au Chocolat (*L'Escargot*) . . . . 68
Orange Custard with Fresh Fruit
  (*Printer's Row*) . . . . . . . . . . . . . . 141
Puff Pastry (*Chez Paul*) . . . . . . . . . . . 43
Rice Pudding (*Cape Cod Room*) . . . . . 27
Ricotta Cheese Cake (*Sogni Dorati*) . . . 151
Sesame Cookies (*Three Happiness*) . . . 167
Strawberries Romanoff (*Chez Paul*) . . . 45
White Chocolate Mousse (*George's*) . . . 75
Yoshi's Fresh Pear Charlotte (*Yoshi's
  Café*) . . . . . . . . . . . . . . . . . . . . . 183

## Entrées

Baked Grouper (*The Bakery*) . . . . . . . . 15
Chicken with Garlic Sauce (*House of
  Hunan*) . . . . . . . . . . . . . . . . . . . . 93
Chile Rellenos *Meson del Lago*) . . . . . 124
Croustade of Bay Scallops with Saffron
  and Julienne Vegetables (*Tango*) . . . 157
Five Spice Beef (*House of Hunan*) . . . . 91
Fricassee de Lapin Aux Racines
  (*L'Escargot*) . . . . . . . . . . . . . . . . . 66
Grilled Rouget with Fresh Tomato
  Sauce and Anchovy Butter (*Yoshi's
  Café*) . . . . . . . . . . . . . . . . . . . . . 180
Le Grenadin de Veau "Normade"
  (*Truffles*) . . . . . . . . . . . . . . . . . . 174
Lobster à la Newburg (*Cape Cod
  Room*) . . . . . . . . . . . . . . . . . . . . 26

# RECIPE INDEX

Mahi-Mahi Amandine *Nick's Fishmarket)* .............. 131
Medallions of Veal with Ginger and Lime *(Printers Row)* ......... 139
Roast Fillet of Peppered Pork *(Lexander)* ................. 113
Roast Duck with Fresh Melon *(The Consort)* ............... 50
Rolled Pheasant, Pinenuts and Cabbage *(Jovan)* .............. 102
Salmon en Croute *(Chez Paul)* ...... 43
Sautéed Veal Chop Capriccio *(Georges)* ................. 74
Sogni Dorati Duck *(Sogni Dorati)* .... 148
Spicy Szechwan Snails *(House of Hunan)* ................ 92
Steamed Lake Trout *(Gordon)* ..... 82
Steamed Salmon and Scallops with Capellini *(Arnie's)* .......... 6
Veal Cricket *(Cricket's)* ............. 58
Yu Hsing Chee Pien *(House of Hunan)* .................. 93
Willow Beef *(House of Hunan)* ....... 94

## Pasta, Rice

Pasta Salad *(Sogni Dorati)* ......... 147
Fettucine with Prosciutto, Peas and Cream *(Georges)* .......... 74
Linguini Primavera Salad *(Cricket's)* ................. 55
Vegetable Ravioli *(Printer's Row)* .... 137

## Salad Dressings

Arnie's Dressing *(Arnie's)* .......... 5
Basil Vinaigrette *(Cape Cod Room)* .... 23
Buttermilk Dressing *(Lexander)* ...... 115
Chez Paul Dressing *(Chez Paul)* ..... 41

Goat Cheese and Yogurt Cream Dressing *(The Consort)* .......... 50
Jovan Dressing *(Jovan)* ........... 104
Pasta Salad Dressing *(Lexander)* ..... 110
Pesto Dressing *(Cricket's)* .......... 56
Raspberry Vinaigrette *(Gordon)* ..... 84
Tomato Dressing *(Chestnut Street Grill)* ..................... 31
Vinaigrette Dressing *(Cricket's)* ..... 60
Walnut Oil Dressing *(Truffles)* ...... 173

## Salads

Arnie's Salad *(Arnie's)* ............. 5
Butterleaf Lettuce with Carrot Strings *(The Consort)* ........... 49
Chez Paul Salad *(Chez Paul)* ........ 41
Chinese Cabbage Salad *(Lexander)* ... 115
Coleslaw *(Cape Cod Room)* ........ 25
Cucumber and Onion Salad *(Gordon)* ................... 84
Jovan Dinner Salad *(Jovan)* ........ 104
Noodle Salad *(House of Hunan)* ................. 90
Orange Salad *(Meson del Lago)* ...... 122
Salad Mimosa *(Tango)* ............ 156
Shrimp and Crabmeat Salad *(Chestnut Street Grill)* ........... 31
Spinach Salad with Roquefort *(Yoshi's Café)* ................ 182
Truffles Salade Maison *(Truffles)* ..... 172

## Sauces and Special Seasonings

Anchovy Butter *(Yoshi's Café)* ....... 181
Bechamel Sauce *(Gordon)* .......... 80
Beurre Rouge *(Arnie's)* ............. 7
Bouquet Garni *(Chez Paul)* ......... 42

# RECIPE INDEX

Bordelaise Sauce *(Chez Paul)* . . . . . . . 40
Brandy Sauce *(Lexander)* . . . . . . . . . 114
Brown Sauce *(Chez Paul)* . . . . . . . . . 40
Caramel Sauce *(Lexander)* . . . . . . . . 117
Chef's Salt *(The Bakery)* . . . . . . . . . . 116
Chianti and Rosemary Sauce
   *(Sogni Dorati)* . . . . . . . . . . . . . . 149
Cioppino Sauce *(Chestnut Street
   Grill)* . . . . . . . . . . . . . . . . . . . . . . 34
Demi-Glaze *(Cricket's)* . . . . . . . . . . . 59
Español Sauce *(Lexander)* . . . . . . . . 112
Fresh Tomato Sauce *(Yoshi's Café)* . . . . 181
Hollandaise Sauce *(Gordon)* . . . . . . . 80
Hot Herb Butter *(The Bakery)* . . . . . . 16
Lemon Butter Sauce *(Nick's
   Fishmarket)* . . . . . . . . . . . . . . . . 129
Mornay Sauce *(Cricket's)* . . . . . . . . . 59
Mushroom Duxelle *(Cricket's)* . . . . . 58
Pheasant Juice *(Jovan)* . . . . . . . . . . 103
Sauce Louis *(The Bakery)* . . . . . . . . . 17
Tomato Butter *(Printer's Row)* . . . . . 138
Tomato Soy Sauce *(Gordon)* . . . . . . 83

## Soup

Black Bean Soup
   *(Meson del Lago)* . . . . . . . . . . . . 123
Boston Clam Chowder *(Cape Cod
   Room)* . . . . . . . . . . . . . . . . . . . . 24
Brie Soup "Jean Lafont" *(Jovan)* . . . . 102
Clam Chowder *(Nick's Fishmarket)* . . . 130
Cauliflower Soup *(Arnie's)* . . . . . . . . 4
Cauliflower Soup *(The Bakery)* . . . . . 14
Cioppino *(Chestnut Street Grill)* . . . . . 33
Consommé Chantilly or Milanaise
   *(Chez Paul)* . . . . . . . . . . . . . . . . 42
Cream of Chili Soup *(Lexander)* . . . . 111
Hot and Sour Soup *(House of
   Hunan)* . . . . . . . . . . . . . . . . . . . 89
Mussel Chowder *(Gordon)* . . . . . . . 80
Mussel Soup *(Yoshi's Café)* . . . . . . . 179
Senegalese Soup *(Cricket's)* . . . . . . . 56

## Stock

Chicken Broth *(Cricket's)* . . . . . . . . . 57
Fish Stock *(Chez Paul)* . . . . . . . . . . . 47
Fish Stock *(Yoshi's Café)* . . . . . . . . . 180
Veal Stock *(Gordon)* . . . . . . . . . . . . 81

## Vegetables and Side Dishes

Anise Carrots *(Sogni Dorati)* . . . . . . . 150
Carrots à La Ricci *(Nick's
   Fishmarket)* . . . . . . . . . . . . . . . . 132
Celery Knob Remoulade *(The
   Bakery)* . . . . . . . . . . . . . . . . . . . 17
Hot Cabbage, à la Reims *(Cricket's)* . . . 60
Sautéed Vegetables *(Printer's Row)* . . . 140
Vegetable Garnish *(L'Escargot)* . . . . . 67

*187*

## *ABOUT THE AUTHOR*

Barbara Grunes is well known as an effusive and popular cooking teacher/food writer here in the Chicago area. She began her career as an educational psychologist. Eventually she transferred her interest of food into her successful second career and now is a nationally published food writer. Barbara studied food with the masters in this country. She is a contributing food writer for the North Shore Magazine and travels extensively writing articles. Grunes is the author of eight cookbooks and is a consultant to the food industry. Barbara lives in Glencoe, Illinois, with her husband and youngest daughter.

# DINING IN–THE GREAT CITIES
*A Collection of Gourmet Recipes from the Finest Chefs in the Country*

Each book contains gourmet recipes for complete meals from the chefs of 21 great restaurants.

| | | | | |
|---|---|---|---|---|
| ___ | Dining In–Baltimore . . . . . . . . . . . . | $7.95 | ___ Dining In–Monterey Peninsula . . . . . . | $7.95 |
| ___ | Dining In–Boston (Revised) . . . . . . . . | 8.95 | ___ Dining In–Philadelphia . . . . . . . . . . | 8.95 |
| ___ | Dining In–Chicago, Vol. II . . . . . . . . . | 8.95 | ___ Dining In–Phoenix . . . . . . . . . . . . . | 8.95 |
| ___ | Dining In–Chicago, Vol. III . . . . . . . . | 8.95 | ___ Dining In–Pittsburgh (Revised) . . . . . | 7.95 |
| ___ | Dining In–Cleveland . . . . . . . . . . . . | 8.95 | ___ Dining In–Portland . . . . . . . . . . . . | 7.95 |
| ___ | Dining In–Dallas (Revised) . . . . . . . . | 8.95 | ___ Dining In–St. Louis . . . . . . . . . . . . | 7.95 |
| ___ | Dining In–Denver . . . . . . . . . . . . . . | 7.95 | ___ Dining In–San Francisco, Vol. II (Spring '83) | 8.95 |
| ___ | Dining In–Hawaii . . . . . . . . . . . . . . | 8.95 | ___ Dining In–Seattle, Vol. III . . . . . . . . | 8.95 |
| ___ | Dining In–Houston, Vol. II . . . . . . . . | 7.95 | ___ Dining In–Sun Valley . . . . . . . . . . . | 7.95 |
| ___ | Dining In–Kansas City (Revised) . . . . | 8.95 | ___ Dining In–Toronto . . . . . . . . . . . . . | 8.95 |
| ___ | Dining In–Los Angeles (Revised) . . . . | 8.95 | ___ Dining In–Vail . . . . . . . . . . . . . . . | 8.95 |
| ___ | Dining In–Manhattan . . . . . . . . . . . . | 8.95 | ___ Dining In–Vancouver, B.C. . . . . . . . . | 8.95 |
| ___ | Dining In–Milwaukee . . . . . . . . . . . . | 8.95 | ___ Dining In–Washington, D.C. . . . . . . . | 8.95 |
| ___ | Dining In–Minneapolis/St. Paul, Vol. II . | 8.95 | | |

☐ Check (✔) here is you would like to have a different Dining In–Cookbook sent to you once a month. Payable by MasterCard or VISA. Returnable if not satisfied.

*Please include $1.00 postage and handling for each book.*

☐ Payment enclosed    $ _____ (total amount)

☐ Charge to:

VISA # _____ Exp. Date _____

MasterCard # _____ Exp. Date _____

Signature _____

Name _____

Address _____

City _____ State _____ Zip _____

SHIP TO (if other than name and address above):

Name _____

Address _____

City _____ State _____ Zip _____

# PEANUT BUTTER PUBLISHING
2445 76th Avenue S.E. ▪ Mercer Island, WA 98040 ▪ (206) 236-1982

CHIC
9/83